Color in American Newspapers

Edited by Mario R. Garcia and Don Fry

A Poynter Institute Graphics & Design Center Report

Acknowledgments

Special thanks to the following individuals and their organizations who contributed enormously to this book:

Nanette Bisher, the Orange County *Register*.

Randy Stano, *The Miami Herald*, and his artists Phill Flanders and Ana Lense.

Mike Peters, *The Dayton Daily News*, and staffers Ed Henninger and Ted Pitts. We are grateful to Tribune Media Services for allowing us permission to use the Mother Goose & Grimm strip created by Peters.

Jorge Vargas, *El Mundo* (San Juan, Puerto Rico).

The Amiga advertisement appearing on page 12 is copyrighted by Commodore Electronics Limited and is reprinted with permission.

The Josten's advertisement, also on page 12, is reprinted with permission.

For Nelson Poynter (1903-1978),
a pioneer in newspaper color and design

Table of Contents

How
To Use
This Book

Don Fry

First of all, take everything in this book with a grain of salt, except this sentence: "We know very little for certain about how people react to color." Researchers know little about the psychology and physiology of color, and even less about color in newspapers. This book attempts to fill some of that gap, but it represents only the beginning of a quest for information vital to the future of the newspaper industry.

We conceived this book as a "starter kit" for anyone who wants to know more about newspaper color, especially for newspaper executives considering starting up or improving their own color capability. The audience includes professional designers, graphics personnel, publishers, editors, reporters interested in graphics, freelance artists, researchers, professors, and students, among others. I have heavily edited the experts who speak in this volume to make their remarks accessible to the widest possible audience. The book tells what we know about color in newspapers right now (October 1986), and provides the means to follow up on any of the information or opinions.

In the first report, Robert Chestnut reviews published research. Most of the research he describes belongs to advertising color, and was conducted with advertising applications in mind. Advertising researchers may frame their questions in terms inappropriate for newspapers. News-editorial people should evaluate the conclusions with skepticism, and should not attempt to apply them to newspaper concerns without making adjustments for the differences in the two media.

Next follow success stories from three newspapers generally acknowledged as leaders in color. The four authors give useful advice in anecdotal form. They speak from management perspectives, ranging from decision-making at the highest level to nuts-and-bolts. Two themes emerge: the importance of quality and the need for each paper to create its own color identity.

The heart of this book reports the research findings from The Poynter Institute color project conducted by Drs. Mario Garcia and Robert Bohle. This study attempted to test for the first time the mechanisms by which color guides the eye of the reader over the page. It also surveys readers' attitudes toward color in newspapers, and finds them quite favorable. But this finding must be applied with great care. A casual reader might assume that if people like color, newspapers should drench themselves in it. But first we need to find out *why* readers like color, and exactly what they like about it. I suspect that readers like the way color can organize the disparate elements on the page, helping them to sort out what goes with what.

The last report describes research conducted in Richmond, Virginia on the effects of color on rack sales and on coupon redemption. The results ran against some expectations, and they do *not* suggest that color can increase sales. These tests need some new questions and larger samples before we apply them generally.

Then Mario Garcia distills the findings of his research and experience as a designer into a series of general tips for the application of color in newspapers. Mario tells us how to dance the color samba without splashing our papers with what he calls "the Carmen Miranda look." We hope these tips will inspire others to share their own tricks.

The bibliography seeks to serve all the audiences of this book. We have included all the best books and articles we know about, as well as some marginal materials that may have some use. Even the least intelligent study or ephemeral article may suggest useful pathways and techniques to researchers and practitioners. We invite readers to contribute entries they find useful which we might have missed, so that the Poynter Institute library can keep a running bibliography on newspaper color.

Ideally, a book describing the state of the art in newspaper color should set an example of the best color repro- duction. We have attempted to reproduce our supplied samples with the highest quality, but our sources vary widely in their technology, color capability, and even staff talent. Some of the older original pages have yellowed, and some no longer exist in paper form, requiring us to print from archival transparencies. All these factors affect the appearance of even high quality reproduction.

Finally, I wish to thank those people who helped with this book, especially the authors, our director Robert Haiman, and my colleagues Billie Keirstead, Joyce Olson, and Cary Waulk. The Institute hopes that this slim volume will spark further research on newspaper color, not just by scientific investigators, but also by newspaper professionals, as we all work together to improve our craft.

Don Fry is an associate director of The Poynter Institute for Media Studies, teaching in the Writing and Ethics Centers. He edits Best Newspaper Writing and consults widely as a writing coach.

About This Book

Robert J. Haiman

During the first week of November 1985, 75 journalists, scholars, and technical experts gathered at The Poynter Institute for Media Studies in St. Petersburg for a symposium on the artistry of color in newspapers. They came at the invitation of the Institute to celebrate the first 25 years of regular use of color in American newspapers. For three days the discussion ranged broadly over the extraordinary impact of the introduction of color on daily journalism. The participants listened to success stories, commiserated about occasional misfires and failures, and heard the results of a new research study on the effects of color on individual newspaper readers. They learned that color has enormous impact, that it can dramatize and help explain the news, that it can sell newspapers and advertising space, and that there is still much to learn.

The following is excerpted from my opening remarks to the seminar participants.

Robert J. Haiman
President and Managing Director
The Poynter Institute

When I was an editor at the *St. Petersburg Times*, working with color was one of the more enjoyable things I did in the newsroom. I can recall vividly the day, more than 10 years ago, when we installed our first laser color scanner. George Sweers, the director of news illustration, said to me, "Bob, it's the first one in North America at a newspaper." Now, more than 100 newspapers have scanners, more are being added every week, and the *Times* is well into its second scanner. (And if I know George Sweers, he is already plotting to find a way to get a third.)

The Newspaper Advertising Bureau predicts that, by the year 2010, all American dailies will offer high-quality process color every day. A number of years ago, when I was getting ready to work on a big layout on a major story (in those days, about five color pictures), I thought to myself that someday I wanted to be the first editor to put out a newspaper in which every single photo, even the one-column head shots and the half-column thumbnails, would all be in color. I didn't get to do that. Maybe one of the editors who attended the color seminar will accomplish that feat one day soon, if *USA Today* hasn't done it already.

Anyone considering color should keep several caveats in mind. First, I believe it will do newspapers no good to use the muscle power of the new technology to ram through a paper in which every photo is in color unless the quality of those photos is better than some I still see.

Second, I believe it will do newspapers no good to print color photographs of excellent quality unless those photos are also truly journalistic and help to tell the story of the day's news.

Finally, I believe it will do newspapers the least good if we are ever tempted to use the power of our new scanners to distort the truth of the scenes our photographers have recorded. For if we ever do that, our readers (who are always smarter than we think they are) will quickly discover that pictures *can* lie, and that newspapers with their new machines can *make* them lie. And we will destroy our credibility, which already bears a burden much heavier than it can easily carry.

1

The 3-Color Samba

Mario R. Garcia

Thinking of color, one sees images of bright hot air balloons, daisies, and the red-white-and-blue that says "American." Thinking of a favorite color, one sees a flashing hue of that one color that has managed to paint our subconscious. For me, that color is blue, my favorite long before it became a signature color for *USA Today*'s nameplate and the legion of imitating newspapers that wear it as a proud hat. It is difficult to imagine television without color, and the same is true of the cover of *Time* magazine, with its ever-present red frame around the cover image.

Now think, "color in newspapers," or "newspaper color," and even "colored newspapers." All three phrases make sense. In fact, any discussion of color as it pertains to newspapers could accommodate each of those phrases.

Color Newspapers

Some newspapers obviously put tremendous emphasis on color. You could say they put "color" before "newspaper." Color in this case becomes a dominant force without which the newspaper would lose its image, a naked, wandering soul, unrecognized and totally out of its element.

For these newspapers, a mandate has come from the publisher to go with color daily, regardless of the news that day and how it should be presented. The news will get painted, usually with bold strokes of the brush. Like anything mandatory, this approach to color becomes dictatorial, for the page designer as well as for the reader.

"Quality is built in, not colored on," wrote Robert Lockwood and Edward Miller in 1984. Journalistic quality means measuring color with the same yardstick as other graphic elements: its functionalism, and how it helps to communicate the messages on the page.

Newspaper Color

In the category of "newspaper color," we find those newspapers that put "newspaper" before "color." Color adds interesting touches, and may assist in moving the reader through that wonderland of type, white space, and images we serve up daily. But color does not become a dominant visual element. I feel comfortable dealing with newspapers that put "color" after "newspaper," not as an afterthought, but as a secondary element.

Seven years ago, the first edition of my book *Contemporary Newspaper Design* did not include a whole chapter on designing with color, as the second edition does. My initial instinct was to write a sentence that sounded something like this:

"Newspapers do not need color to do what they do best. In fact, if color has not been technically perfected, it is best to steer clear of it. Black and white are colors too, and the combination of the two shades is what we associate with newsprint and newspapers generally."

Well, that sentence did not get too far, even in 1979. Two of the manuscript reviewers, whose advice I still value, considered the statement too strong and arbitrary. I did not agree, but thought about it for a long time, and finally struck the sentence out of the manuscript. Today I still agree that it is better to have a black-and-white newspaper if color reproduction is not the best that it can be, but I have mellowed somewhat. There are new rainbows in my head, some of which project beautiful newspaper pages, and they are in color. I think of those front pages covering the Space Shuttle tragedy in 1986, of many food and fashion pages that rival the stuff we could only expect to see in magazines and posters, the many maps and graphs that use color to guide us through facts and figures. These are all examples of color used functionally, where the hues enhance the information and present it with clarity and visual appeal. Yes, newspaper color is a more intelligent design choice today than it was in 1979, or back in 1457, when historians tell us the first color was produced in what we may refer to as mass communications. It was a plate in a printed religious book, using blue and red on the woodcut of a monk at prayer.

Newspaper color today has advanced tremendously since an American newspaper, *The Milwaukee Journal*, ran a color bar overlay on its front page of January 5, 1891, to mark the inauguration of a new governor. It was blue and red over black.

Despite these advances, vast as they are, we have not gone far enough. We asked a sampling of American and Canadian editors how they rated color in newspapers on this continent. On a scale of 1-to-10, the average was 4.2.

Colored Newspapers

Such low regard for color use in newspapers probably comes from a third category, what I call "colored newspapers," the ones that evoke laughter when shown in seminar sessions. These are the newspapers where the editors, who never got beyond the Crayola stage in elementary school, suddenly arm themselves with a box of 36 crayons and lash out, samurai style, with yellows deeper than those on New York City taxicabs, greens reminiscent of laundry detergent boxes, and purples (usually for a food page devoted to blueberries) that look as if a bunch of grapes had been mashed on the page. The combinations, which sometimes include all three of these loud colors at the top of page one, create what I describe as the "Carmen Miranda Look."

Carmen Miranda was a Brazilian musical star who conquered Hollywood during the 1940s and 50s with her multi-colored, tutti-frutti headgear. She is gone now, alas, but her revival echoes daily on the front pages of newspapers across the land. When Carmen created her look, she knew what she was doing. Every pineapple and banana and peach and plum and orange and kumquat that escalated to crown her outrageous hats created a certain effect, by her design.

When many newspapers put on their Carmen Miranda hats, however, the process is often less selective, and definitely more hurried. A typical scenario goes something like this: as page one is finished, the editor realizes there is color available, and presto, a yellow, a pink, and a purple dance a three-color samba into the promos.

Color in newspapers, as well as in the headgear of musical stars, needs planning and coordination.

That planned coordination is what this book is all about. First, we must remind our readers that this is not a textbook with answers to all their questions. It is not a primer on color use. It is an attempt to capture the highlights of our November 1985 Color Symposium at The Poynter Institute, to organize the thoughts and insights of experts in the industry who shared their knowledge with us during the three-day program.

Most importantly, this book attempts to put color in American newspapers in perspective by:

• Increasing awareness of the importance of color from the perspective of the readers, seeing color as a reality of the world around us.

• Profiling successful newspapers such as *USA Today*, the *St. Petersburg Times*, and the Orange County (Cal.) *Register*, all of which have devoted considerable efforts to make color use a part of the plan, and not an afterthought.

• Revealing how color affects eye movement on the page, as tested during The Poynter Institute's research project, conceived and carried out exclusively for presentation in the Color Symposium.

• Articulating how research findings can become applicable design strategies to help us all make better use of newspaper color.

• Providing a selected bibliography on aspects of color and its newspaper applications.

We envision this book as the type of publication that you can easily read in one sitting, the type of book that you can underline with your yellow accent pen, and then take it back to the newsroom or art department to help you the next time you design with color. We also see it as a quick introduction to starting up or expanding the use of color. We have made it accessible to design experts and general managers alike.

If time allows, put an old Carmen Miranda flick on the VCR and get all that tutti-frutti stuff out of your system.

After a good night's sleep, you too will probably samba into the newsroom the next day ready to apply "newspaper color."

Mario R. Garcia is associate director in charge of the Graphics and Design Center at The Poynter Institute for Media Studies, professor of mass communications at the University of South Florida, and visiting professor of graphic arts at Syracuse University. The author of Contemporary Newspaper Design, Garcia is a consultant to newspapers around the world and was a Fulbright Scholar in newspaper design in 1984-85.

2 The Myth & Magic of Color

Robert W. Chestnut

Color is an ever present part of our daily experience, the world around us. We rarely escape color, even in darkness. We constantly and systematically respond to color. Although the effects of color can be profound, more often than not, we are barely aware of color's influence on our behavior. It is a natural, routine part of our existence, with a meaning that is hard to capture or express in words.

From my background in psychology and advertising research, I want to introduce the many complex ways in which color enters into our lives. All of us, in our own ways, are already experts in color. Consider how early our training begins.

Research indicates that at two months of age, the infant has established and is practicing color perception. This development occurs before the primary visual system is yet in place, before the eye can recognize shape or organization, and before visual acuity gets any better than 20/600. At this time in the infant's life, when, as William James observed, the world is a "blooming, buzzing confusion," color is seen and has impact. That impact stays with the child, and develops quickly at the age of four months into distinct color preferences. As soon as speech appears, that impact is reflected in one of the most stable and meaningful sets of concepts in language: the four basic hues of red, yellow, green, and blue.

By the time we are adults, we have accumulated rich, finely textured histories of color experience. We are, by most standards, experts in color. Yet, when asked, we can say surprisingly little about the nature of our experience or expertise. A key point in my remarks is the simple realization that the challenge facing research is not to know more about color. It is, paradoxically, to know more about what all of us already seem to have learned about color. We need to probe deeper into what for us is almost second nature: the subjective experience of color.

Like most things that we fail to understand adequately but somehow know to be important, color has come to be associated over time with a long list of "mysterious" effects. Some of these effects are in reality nothing more than popular fictions or myths. Others contain a kernel of truth, pointing in the direction of what might be called the true magic of color's influence. Fundamental to progress in our understanding of color must be the separation of these myths from color's magic.

My presentation is structured along these lines. By way of a brief overview, I will consider four topics:

• The fundamental presence of color in our lives, particularly our mental lives.

• The myths surrounding color, including the various ways in which color is thought to affect us, but in all likelihood does not.

• The magic of color's influence, cases where, through research, we have begun to isolate color's effects.

• An understanding of color by summarizing research findings.

I am not going to be concentrating

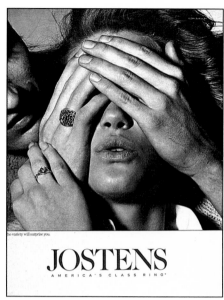

FIG. 2A and FIG. 2B. Recently, ads for such products as the Amiga Computer and Josten's class rings have selectively removed color to take the reader back to the days of black and white. But notice how the ads also build positive associations between color and the product to emphasize key benefits.

on the sheer visual experience of color. I would like instead to stimulate your mind and the way you think about color. As I have just pointed out, it is not color itself but the mental response to color that interests us here.

To reinforce this point, reflect for a moment on the words of Johannes Itten, an authority on the creative use of color: "The effects of color must be experienced and understood not just visually...but psychologically and symbolically." This is not a quotation from a fellow psychologist, but rather from an artist who, although he lived and breathed the artistry of color, nevertheless realized and made use of the fact that color's impact happens within. More than a visual experience, color is information. It is meaning. It is a call to action.

A dvertising has long made use of this fact. Ads with color outperform those without; they have a psychological impact on their audience. Research established this effect quite early in the industry's development. In 1913, Walter Dill Scott concluded that "bright colors impress us more than dull ones." To help establish this point, he conducted a study of the reasons for noting and responding to magazine advertisements. Color ranked high, even above interest in buying the product.

Today, such research continues. A recent study sponsored by the newspaper industry, for example, finds improved audience response attributable to color on a number of levels: awareness, reading, etc. We have reached the point where the simple observation that color has impact is one of our most stable and time-tested results. We have also reached the point where we must in all honesty ask ourselves: is this progress?

Creatively, advertising has made great strides in the sophistication with which it employs color. Consider ads such as some of the recent ones for the Amiga Computer or Dr. Pepper. In a world of color television, these two ads selectively remove color to take us emotionally back to the days of black and white. At the same time, they build positive associations between color and the product to em-

phasize key benefits, such as color graphics or the uniqueness of taste. Armed with advanced video and computer technology, advertising will most likely continue this progress in creative approach.

Research is challenged to keep pace. It needs to end its fixation with the strategy of color (Do we use it?) and to start to address the tactics of color (How do we use it, and with what effects?). One creative director recently pointed to an increasing role within advertising for what he called the "sensory engineer." Advertising research can fill this role, and is in the process of doing so. Clearly, as a first step, researchers must consider in more detail the fundamental presence of color in our mental lives.

The Fundamental Presence of Color

The existence of color in the physical world is a matter of precise scientific description and inquiry. Though I need not go into any great detail regarding this science and its findings, it is the starting point for our subjective experience of color. We should consider certain of its concepts.

One of color science's more interesting representations of our experience, at least as it starts out in the physical world, is the color solid, a three-dimensional concept of color structured around the properties of hue, intensity, and saturation.

"Hue," or "wavelength," is what many of us naively refer to as "color." We define it as the crest-to-crest distance of the light wave, stretching from relatively long infrared waves to the much shorter ultraviolet end of the spectrum. In terms of visible light, we are talking about a distance of approximately 1/33,000 of an inch for the color red to 1/67,000 of an inch for the color blue.

"Intensity" refers to the magnitude or quantity of light present. Visually, this property ranges from black through various shades of gray to white.

Finally, there is "saturation." A color becomes saturated as it mixes with the presence of white light or intensity. Saturation implies that colors become more or less vivid to our senses.

The most striking characteristic of this color solid is its interactive complexity. Taken together, these three dimensions create up to 7.5 million potential, subtle variations of experience.

The human mind confronts the full range of this experience and translates or recodes it to 350,000 just noticeable differences (JNDs). By two months of age, the mind has reviewed these 350,000 JNDs and has decided on four specific, primary or "focal" colors on which to concentrate its attention. But this is just the beginning, the reduction of the physical world to a more manageable and structured input. Now, the real work begins. For the rest of our lives, we are engaged in a task of constantly elaborating these simple four colors into a full range of color experience.

By four months of age, we have achieved relatively stable color preferences (which remain with us as adults), and are well on our way to a conceptual set of eight to 11 colors: red, orange, yellow, green, blue, purple, pink, brown, black, white, and gray.

With language, these concepts come to be described by a color vocabulary numbering upward of 4,000 words. Behind these words stand millions of associations. Consider the ways in which these associations orient us in our daily lives, with clothing, with food, with products, etc.

Research by Berlin and Kay highlights the fundamental presence of these associations, not just at a personal level, but also at a cultural level. Color concepts and their verbal/nonverbal implications have not always been there for the human mind to work with. They have evolved with culture to help us manage the more sophisticated demands of life. If we go back to "primitive" languages and cultures, we find the meaning and application of color limited according to the needs of the culture. Color is a tool. And in today's world, it is an increasingly sophisticated and precise one.

Myths Surrounding Color

However, understanding of this tool is limited. Our understanding remains shrouded, even today, in myth and folklore. Birren notes: "It is perhaps a mistaken notion that man in his love of color was impelled by some aesthetic urge.... The greatest weight of evidence points to the fact

"The effects of color must be experienced and understood not just visually...but psychologically and symbolically."

Johannes Itten

> "It is perhaps a mistaken notion that man in his love of color was impelled by some aesthetic urge. The greatest weight of evidence points to the fact that color was involved with the supernatural..."
>
> **Faber Birren**

that color was involved with the supernatural."

The supernatural qualities of color emerge in a number of areas. In religion, color has a powerful role, especially in terms of hues: yellow in the Orient, green in the Middle East, and blue/red in the western world. In medicine, color has been tied to everything from the alchemists' use of gemstones to treatment by colored lights in the 19th century. In art, color is often more than beauty; it is a spiritual statement. In the Book of Kells and in the stained glass windows of Chartres Cathedral, color transcends the visual experience.

Fortunately, many of the more damaging myths have passed into history. We no longer treat pneumonia, for example, with alternating blue and yellow lights. The remaining myths are now more symbol than substance.

But all our misconceptions have not been dispelled. Many are still present, and only serve to confuse the discussion of color's effects. In this category, we still find color linked to:

• emotional manipulation, e.g., red light as a sexual and seductive influence;

• temperature control, e.g., color as a means of increasing or decreasing body temperature;

• personality, using color preferences to establish basic traits;

• and productivity, the impact of color on work output.

Folklore exists regarding these points, but little real research evidence. My favorite example is Knute Rockne's painting his football stadium's locker rooms in different colors, that is having his home team retire to fire-engine red quarters at half-time, and his opponents to deep sea blue. Such stories are great for conversation, but they have no real value in understanding color's influence.

The Magic of Color's Influence

For such understanding, we need to turn to the experimental literature on color. A computer-based search covering the past 10 years of research evidence was made, and the findings were systematically reviewed to highlight consistent and interesting results. Over 150 articles were evaluated. What follows is a summary of experimental findings on the subjective experience of color. To organize the discussion, the findings are grouped into four areas. Each of these categories represents a general characteristic of color's influence.

1. Color's influence is subtle.

At a perceptual level, color works

in a number of interesting ways. One of these ways concerns our ability to use color actively without a great deal of conscious effort or attention to its actual presence. A simple experiment on "wayfinding" involved people orienting themselves in a new environment, in this case, an office building. The subjects performed before and after a repainting of the office space that provided a variety of color-coded cues for establishing their physical location. Performance in finding one's way about the building improved dramatically with the addition of these cues, as one might expect. Significantly, however, the subjects lacked any awareness of the presence or use of color information in wayfinding.

Another mechanism underlying color's influence is called "multiple coding." For example, we can demonstrate "interference effects," by picturing the word "RED" printed in the contrasting color green (Fig. 2C). It is impossible to look at this word without receiving multiple meanings and hesitating over an interpretation. Color transmits to us simultaneously at a verbal and nonverbal level, one of the reasons it fixes itself so well in our memory for later identification.

FIG. 2C

Finally, color is imagery. It forms subtle associations that intertwine with our other senses to heighten our subjective experience of the world around us. Color "hearing," for example, is the tendency of most people (60 percent of those tested) to see color as they relax, close their eyes, and listen to music.

2. Color's meaning is rich.

Although its influence is subtle,

color's richness of meaning is strong and obvious. In the following simple quiz, notice how readily the strong emotional associations come to mind:

Angry: "See ———."
Sad: "Feel ————."
Scared: "———— streak."
Trustworthy: "True ————."
Envy: "———— with."

In the realm of product packaging and consumer behavior, color has no less powerful associations. Color association even has ramifications in the law. A landmark case in the federal courts, Union Carbide vs. BASF, actually rules on the competitive need for the color yellow in the antifreeze market.

Research on our "semantic space" for color, that is, the dimensions along which we define color's meaning, shows three separate responses to color. Color impacts directly on our evaluation of good versus bad. It does so in highly specific and learned ways. No one color always produces a positive reaction; rather, a color which seems most appropriate to the situation is judged best.

Color also means activity. Red, as you might expect, lends an active, energetic impression, while blue denotes a passive meaning.

Finally, saturation lends strength. Highly saturated colors imply something more powerful than softer, weaker, less vivid colors.

3. Color's unique leverage acts upon emotion.

Color does alter our physiological state. Systematically, we respond to it on a number of measures of activi-ty. Red tends to mean activity; it also tends to create activity or arousal. Galvanic Skin Response (GSR), blood pressure, respiration, and eye blink all increase under red light condi-tions. On several of these indications, blue has the opposite result.

Arousal of our activity level is a first step in our emotional response to the world around us. One recent theory suggests that our color pref-erences may vary with our emotional condition and arousal level. Given a state of low arousal and an emotional condition of "boredom," we generally seek more active colors such as red to manipulate our arousal level and create "excitement." Given a state of high arousal and an emotional condi-tion of "anxiety," we generally seek more passive colors such as blue to manipulate our arousal level and create "relaxation."

Research has measured such shifts in preference over the course of the day and found an average of from two to four shifts in every five-hour period. Rather than a fixed indication of our personality, color seems to be a better indication of our constantly changing mood states and emotional judgments.

4. Color's meaning is real.

Even though our experience of col-or is subjective, laden with imagery, emotions, and past associations, its personal meaning for us is neverthe-less real. Color's meaning is especial-ly real when it then changes our behavior.

This phenomenon is readily appar-ent in placebo effects in medicine. Research on capsule color substan-tiates certain colors as more "potent" than others, and the placebo effects of such colored capsules are stronger.

In areas other than medicine, perception can become reality. Re-search on political candidates shows that certain color associations, for example, on posters or in political symbols, can lead to candidate pref-erences based on notions of age, honesty, dynamism, and personal at-traction.

Summary

My summary is short because I feel that these various indications of col-or's influence speak for themselves. They point us generally in the direc-tion of continued research, but re-search which is more tailored to the specific and detailed ways in which we use color.

Certainly, color does have magic. It is particularly striking in the ease and subtlety of its use, in the strength of its associations, and in the emotion-al impact of its experience. Creative-ly, we do use color in communications. Practically speaking, we can improve the impact of these communications by understanding better the influ-ence of color on our audiences.

Robert W. Chestnut is vice president and director of research development at Ted Bates Worldwide, Inc. of New York City. Chestnut is actively involved in research systems and innovative techniques to aid strategic and creative decisions. He is a former professor of business at the Grad-uate School of Business at Columbia Uni-versity and was senior vice president and research director for the Advertising Research Foundation.

Questions and Observations

1. Chestnut draws many of his observations from research on advertising, which seeks to attract and persuade. Think about possible conflicts of attraction and persuasion with the desire for "objectivity" in news presentation.

2. Chestnut says, "We have reached the point where the simple observation that color has impact is one of our most stable and time-tested results. We have also reached the point where we must in all honesty ask ourselves: is this progress?" How would you answer his question?

3. Chestnut points to some recent ads that use black and white to remind viewers of earlier days and values. Can we achieve such effects in a newspaper when even the most colorful papers remain mostly black and white? Could we use equivalent techniques, such as printing pictures in sepia?

4. Chestnut seeks to dispel myths such as "red light as a sexual and seductive influence." Yet this myth persists in our culture (especially in bachelor pads) despite the lack of any evidence for its reality in physiology or psychology. Designers can still play off these myths, simply because the public believes in them.

5. The "wayfinding" experiments show us that subjects cannot articulate their experience, especially to describe the mental tools they use unconsciously. This finding suggests the need for very skillful and probing interviewers in color research projects, especially in those concerning newspaper color.

6. Chestnut tells us that "no one color always produces a positive reaction; rather, a color which seems most appropriate to the situation is judged best." How can we design research or even anecdotal testing to discover the means for judging appropriateness to a situation? Culture, especially at a regional level, may play a role here.

7. Chestnut's remarks on the arousing effects of red versus the calming effects of blue seem to conflict with his skepticism toward the Knute Rockne anecdote about painting the locker rooms. Maybe the coach had a point after all!

8. Politicians use color associations in their ads. How can editors avoid the dangers and temptations of "coloring" information by their choices of colors on news pages?

3

Three Success Stories

We can rarely attribute the success of a newspaper to a single factor, and color is no exception. Readers who have developed strong ties to their newspapers usually cite content, quality of reporting and editing, commitment to overall excellence, and community service.

The following three success stories, however, pertain to excellence in color use. They involve commitments on the part of publishers and editors to enhance the quality of content, reporting, and editing by reproducing the best color available. These editors see color as a tool for improving communications.

The editors of the three newspapers profiled here, *USA Today*, the *St. Petersburg Times*, and the Orange County (Cal.) *Register*, think of their newspapers in terms of color. They describe the tremendous efforts required to achieve success with color, particularly the problems associated with first starting to print it. They each emphasize how maintaining high standards in color use becomes a daily task requiring as much dedication and commitment as that normally given to such areas as good content and reporting.

John S. Garvey
John N. Walston

USA Today is the nation's newspaper. Gannett, the owner of *USA Today*, believes that most forms of media and many new ones (including *USA Today*) will find a successful role in complementary yet competitive ways in the decade of the 1980s. Print media that survive the technological revolution will use new forms of

The color photographs in *USA Today* are produced on two Crosfield laser color scanners that have been programmed to produce color separations tailored for high-quality newspaper reproduction. Typically, color scanners such as Crosfield are found only in high-volume, high-quality engraving shops. But this

FIG. 3A. Crosfield laser scanners, such as those at *USA Today*, usually are found only in high quality engraving shops. With good equipment, newspapers can enjoy color reproduction as good as that done by commercial printers. This scanner divides each inch into more than 1.5 million elements.

technology to communicate more efficiently, more accurately, and more frequently than in the past. The story of how print media will survive is largely the story of *USA Today*.

On September 15, 1982, Gannett began its nationwide phase-in of *USA Today*, the first full-color daily newspaper to be transmitted by satellite. *USA Today* combined technologies developed by *The Wall Street Journal* and *Time* magazine. Today we operate the largest and most sophisticated satellite facsimile network in the world.

trend is changing. Highly-skilled color strippers incorporate the color photographs into the final newspaper pages for transmission to the various print sites. In short, the *USA Today* camera department can produce quality color work equal to the best commercial engraving shops.

To maintain the print quality during transmission to the printing plants, *USA Today* has installed some of the most sophisticated facsimile and satellite equipment anywhere, capable of extremely high resolution scanning. Lasers electronically slice up the page into an extremely complicated grid. Each square inch is divided into more than 1.5 million elements with a scanning resolution of 1,200 lines per inch horizontally by 1,400 lines per inch vertically. This process gives *USA Today* the capability of transmitting color halftones and advertising of magazine quality to all print sites with maximum reproduction.

Once the newspaper page has been photographed and the contact print made, the print is placed on facsimile scanners for the satellite transmission to the sites. As the print revolves on the scanner, a laser reads the image to be printed and translates that image into an electronic signal that can be broadcast by the satellite. Black and white pages can be sent in one transmission. Full color pages require four separate transmissions, one for each of the primary colors: red, blue, yellow, and black. A standard black-and-white newspaper page can be sent in about 3.5 minutes at 800 lines per inch. Each of the individual advertising color transmissions takes 15 minutes at 1,200 lines per inch, which translates into one hour for a full page of advertising. As the page is being scanned at the transmission sites, electronic signals carrying the page data are being sent to the Westar III satellite, for broadcast back simultaneously to all the print sites.

Each printing plant has a five-meter (approximately 16-foot) dish, receiving antenna, and facsimile recorders. The signal is received by the antenna and passed to the facsimile recorders, which are installed in a photographic darkroom. The facsimile recorders translate the electronic signal into a full-page negative, using lasers to expose the film. The full-page negatives are then used to produce offset printing plates. Computers monitor the entire process. They keep track of when pages were transmitted, which print sites

FIG. 3B. Today the modern, high-tech newspaper has computer facilities that look like the command room of the starship Enterprise. This level of technology allows *USA Today* to transmit pages to printing sites nationwide.

require retransmissions, and estimates of the time for the last transmission. Another computer, part of the facsimile broadcast control system, automatically retransmits data to the print site if there are any errors.

Total transmission time for a 40-page newpaper, with three full-color editorial pages and seven full-color advertising pages, spans roughly a 10-hour period from approximately 2:00 p.m. until 11:40 p.m. For East Coast editions, press starts are sched-

uled for midnight, with saleable papers expected within five minutes of the press start.

All the sophisticated facsimile and satellite equipment in the world cannot guarantee quality unless the printing itself is of the highest quality. One of the real successes of *USA Today* has been in its reproduction of full-color, magazine-type advertising and editorial graphics. The printing presses at all *USA Today* print sites, Gannett and non-Gannett alike, have been fine-tuned to commercial printing specifications. In some cases, they were nearly completely rebuilt. Proofs of all ads are printed on a four-unit community offset press in Arlington, using the same inks and newsprint as the *USA Today* printing plants. At each print site, densitometers are used to make sure the printed product exactly matches the ink densities of the advertising proofs and of the editorial color keys provided by headquarters. Seminars have been conducted in conjunction with the Rochester Institute of Technology to train our production personnel in color theory and offset printing techniques. Checklists are used to maintain the printing equipment and to get the presses ready for printing each night. Finally, the printing quality of each site is monitored daily.

The technology employed by *USA Today* is both extensive and sophisticated. Without communications satellite and facsimile transmission, the newspaper would never have gotten off the drawing board. The entire *USA Today* production system, from pre-press to the facsimile and satellite network, to the actual printing plants, was designed with quality as the key goal.

How successful are we in terms of meeting our quality goals? The answer depends on whether you are looking at the long-term or short-term aspects of our efforts. For the most part, our national advertising efforts are compared to the likes of *Time* or *Newsweek*. And much of the time,

such comparison would no doubt be favorable.

There is still more, much more, that can be done to improve quality, reduce variation, and define our standards more clearly. We are looking at different methods of evaluating color, both off-line and on-line. The program for *USA Today*, or for any paper that seeks to produce a quality product, must be ongoing and highly visible within the framework of the organization.

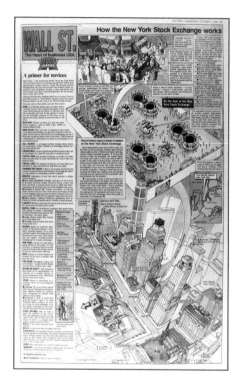

FIG. 3C. Color graphics are an immediate, identifiable element of *USA Today*'s overall design. This spread, explaining the intricacies of Wall Street, emphasizes the colors in the illustration on the bottom half of the page, then accessorizes with other shades in the illustration.

We would like to believe that we have accomplished a few things of merit. We think that we have proved that it is possible for a daily newspaper to produce quality process color consistently, on time, and with reasonable waste. We also think that our approach to quality control at the source has been successful, that standardization of materials and procedures is essential, and that quality by the numbers is both possible and desirable.

New technology continues to grow at *USA Today*. Our most recent addition to the electronic pre-press system comes from Scitex, a software company specializing in electronic imaging systems. The Scitex satellite unit is a portable scanner that can be taken to the site of a major event. It then transmits print-quality digital images back to the Roslyn-based Scitex Pre-sponse 300 computer over normal voice-grade telephone lines.

This system gives us, in effect, a photo bureau network throughout the nation or anywhere in the world. The unit scans 35mm color transparencies, and then digitizes, compresses, and transmits the data in approximately 17 minutes. In Roslyn, the electronic image can be received without significant operator intervention. The photo editors monitor the material, preview the photos for content, quality, and visual impact. The editor selects a photo, and specifies the size and the cropping. The scanner operator calls the photo from a file onto the screen, manipulates the tone curve, does color corrections, and assigns the cropping and sizing data before outputting the image to film on the scanner output unit. So we can go from a 35mm color slide in the field to sized, separated film negatives in minutes rather than hours.

The original satellite prototype was used to transmit photos from the 1984 Summer Olympics and the 1985 Super Bowl. In July 1985, it was used during the National Sports Festival in New Orleans, and more recently for the 1985 World Series, where it performed miraculously.

Now my colleague John Walston will tell you how he and the other talented artists at *USA Today* create such wonderful graphics.

[Walston speaks. Ed.]

One of the wonderful things about *USA Today* is that they give you what you need to work with, and that's important to know. It starts with a commitment, and the commitment has to start at the top. If you don't have the commitment at the top, you will not get the kind of quality you want.

USA Today was very lucky. Al Neuharth said we will print great quality color. And then he stood aside and gave us the money and took all the barriers out of our way to allow us to do it. And I think that is what's wrong with a lot of newspapers in the country. They want to print color, but they don't want to pay for it. As an artist or as an editor, you cannot do a whole lot about printing great color unless it comes from the top.

We were lucky when we started our newspaper because we did not exist in a black-and-white form before. We had the wonderful luxury of sitting down and designing color into our identity. The choice of blue and the *USA Today* logo reversed out in white is part of what *USA Today* is all about.

Many newspapers in the United States have seen *USA Today* print all

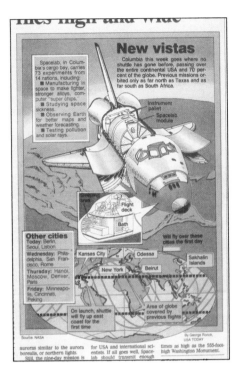

FIG. 3D. This informational graphic introduces color by framing the art work. The same color is picked up for the type boxes, with green dominating the back of the illustration. In addition to its color impact, this graphic also gives the reader substantial information.

FIG. 3E. "Anchored color" is part of *USA Today*'s overall design philosophy, but the colors are also compatible with each other. The blue nameplate gives way to gray boxes on each side. A dominant color from the main photo or illustration at the top echoes at the bottom of the page.

that wonderful, bright, and sometimes garish color. And they say, "That's what we should do." They go back to their papers and start putting color all over it. They put it here. They put it there. They do bright colors. They do this and that.

And finally, they look a lot like *USA Today*. Not intentionally, mind

you. They can't look like *USA Today* because their design is different. But they look like something of an imitation. I would warn you against such imitation unless that's what you want your newspaper to be. In that sense, be careful that the colors you're putting in your paper really work. The Orange County *Register* looks like the Orange County *Register*. It doesn't look like *USA Today*, and yet they print great color. They do a lot with good photography, which becomes a very natural part of their newspaper.

Remember that *USA Today* thought about what it was going to be. It did not have to be redesigned. It planned a unique identity and geared its philosophy around that design. You can't do the same thing because your newspapers already have their own identities. By adding color, you will radically change those identities. So seek out your own identity. Then let color reinforce that identity.

The world is in color, and color is reality. Black and white is not what the real world looks like.

At *USA Today*, we also have a philosophy of what I call "anchored color." We built color into our identity, and therefore you can tell that certain things will always be in color. We insure color presence on our front page every single day and on all our section fronts. You can see the color in the flag and in both ears. There's almost always color in the bottom right hand corner, what we call the "hot corner." And we put color into the middle of the page, which is either the cover story or the major lead article of the day. All that is part of our identity, and we build on it. We want to make sure that when you look at our paper, you know what it is. These practices guarantee a lot of color in our paper. We also live by a basic philosophy: keep it clean and keep it simple.

Graphics

Probably the easiest way to add color to your paper is to use graphics. A lot of graphics makes your paper look colorful and bright. But if you're going to use graphics and color that way, make sure it's packed with information. Make it news. Make sure the readers feel they're getting something substantial, not something frivolous.

On that point, avoid cartoons and frivolous illustrations. You're a newspaper, and you need to transmit the idea to your reader that you are a newspaper. Too often I see people doing cute illustrations or cute cartoons, just slapping them on page one to illustrate a story. And you get a feeling that the paper is not a very serious paper. Make your graphics work for you. Make them news.

Remember that graphics are easier to read in color than they are in black and white. We do a lot of black-and-white graphics at *USA Today*. But black-and-white graphics are a whole lot harder to do. You have to think about more things. Color makes it easier to do graphics. In black and white, you have only a certain number of shades of gray and black. Remember that color is actually easier, but only if you apply it in the right manner.

FIG. 3F. If a color photograph is not available, the editors at *USA Today* incorporate color on the page by using a color portrait, as seen in this example. The portrait is more than just a face; it also moves the reader into the story and adds information.

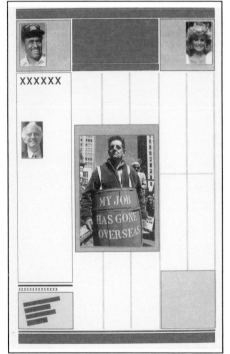

FIG. 3G. This *USA Today* grid shows the anchor positions for color. The strict grid allows color to fall into certain positions, such as the nameplate, ears, the lower left corner "snapshot" and the lower right "hot corner." Familiarity of color placement aids compatibility.

FIG. 3H. Red becomes a dominant element in this sports page. First introduced in the section flag, it then frames the photograph in the middle of the page. Yellow and gray provide good contrast to red, as seen here.

Because we have a "color-only" theory on page one, we have to take special measures. Sometimes we may not have enough photographs in color, so we have developed what we call the "five-hour news portrait." On deadline, we will create a picture that may not look exactly like the person in the news, but will be part of a photo illustration that gives you a feeling for the news of the day.

Photographs

Our policy on section fronts is color photographs only, and that's part of our identity. We didn't want to mix black and white with color on page one, although it's a lot easier to do it that way. Many papers that do run color will mix black and white with color. That's fine for you, but we decided that's not what we were going to do. But it did not make our lives very easy.

In fact, it made it damn tough. It was very hard, not so much in the back parts of the paper, but in the news section. It was very difficult because we had to begin to gear ourselves to thinking color, thinking news, and shooting color, plus deal with the transportation problems of getting from one end of the country to the other, of flying color in. If you wanted to get a picture out of Los Angeles to Washington, D.C. in time to make the press that night, it had to leave Los Angeles by 9 o'clock Pacific time just to make our paper. That's one of the reasons we had so much interest in developing Scitex down the line.

We got a lot of criticism in the beginning about a lot of things. I think a lot of that criticism is fading now, because during the last three years of doing color, we've gotten better at it. And now it doesn't bother you as much.

With our photographs, we try to go for the very strong image, the big image. We try to look for big faces. And so we give a big pull to the page. That big image is part of the identity of *USA Today*. As for criticism of our running photographs too small, we feel we run them in the size they need to be for our newspaper. What you see are images that are very big, while the photograph as a whole may be only a three column photograph. The image of the face would be the same as that in a five column photograph that your paper may have run. We're very consistent about that. And we are looking for news images from that day.

I n our use of spot color, readability of type is the most important thing. Mixing color and type on the same page and mixing color over type can be very tricky. You need to learn a little something about color theory. Remember that light colors come forward, and dark colors recede, just basic things like that.

At *USA Today*, we have a basic policy that 30 percent of the color is either blue or magenta. But we don't go over that limit because it begins to fill in around the words and the

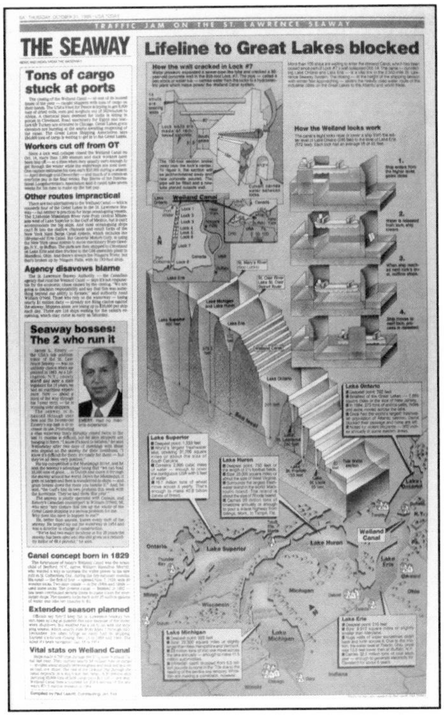

FIG. 3I. Detailed informational graphics need a dominant color (in this case, green), with compatible colors used as accessories. However, the more color used in a supergraphic such as this, the more white space needs to be emphasized somewhere on the page.

characters, and you can't read it very well. So keep your percentages very light over type, and don't go with really heavy colors.

But a lot of people take type (normal size, nine- or 10-point type) and reverse it out of color. Once you've done that, you've walked into a very dangerous area. If your presses don't get it in absolute register, there is no way you can read the type. You've got to watch it very carefully. At *USA Today*, we have a very strict limit about how much white type you can have. When we do use reverse type, we generally do it on an all black base and reverse out of that, not having any color involved.

Remember that black is also a color. We get so carried away with our ability to put color into the newspaper that we forget black can be very effective. In one case, we used a black background to make a picture of Hamilton Jordan pop out of the page and enhance the color there. In another case, we used it as a base for the All-Star page that we do every year for the high schools. The color pictures get more brilliant, and the base holds the page together.

We use colors that you can read through. We use a very small number of colors that way. We don't try to use colors to set moods for stories. I think there's a danger there, that you may be trying to do too much for the reader. You use colors and visual images in graphics to help communicate the in-

FIG. 3J. The many color photographs here, which would make color coordination difficult, require a gray background to cushion the effect of so many different and incompatible hues. This strategy helps with pages that depend on head shots or other multi-art treatments.

formation. But there is no conscious effort to put color tones on certain things to communicate information. In fact, we generally go to the other extreme of avoiding that.

If you're an editorial person, you need to spend a lot of time downstairs in production. We get to know those people. We had every artist on our staff spend at least a week cross-training in the composing room. We sat down there, and we learned the language used in communicating. We're friends. These are the real people who make the quality of art and graphics that you see.

John S. Garvey is vice president of USA Today, with major responsibility for headquarters production and systems operations. He is also involved with USA Weekend operations and Gannett's Four Color Network.

John N. Walston is deputy managing editor for news, USA Today, where he has also served as deputy managing editor for graphics and photography. Mr. Walston has been an executive news editor with the San Jose Mercury News and the Dallas Times Herald.

Questions and Observations

1. Garvey says: "Print media that survive the technological revolution will use new forms of technology to communicate more efficiently, more accurately, and more frequently than in the past. The story of how print media will survive is largely the story of *USA Today*." What other models for high-tech survival can you think of, especially in newspapers?

2. Garvey praises *USA Today* for its "capability of transmitting color half-tones and advertising of magazine quality to all print sites with maximum reproduction." Is magazine quality an appropriate standard for newspapers? What other standards might they aspire to?

3. Garvey describes *USA Today*'s ongoing training and quality control, two themes that dominate this book. How can managers keep these two necessities at the front of their concern and high in their budgets?

4. Walston praises his superiors because "they give you what you need to work with.... It starts with a commitment, and the commitment has to start at the top." How can designers and editors encourage such commitment to providing the right tools and people? How can top managers know what they need to provide, both in terms of funds and encouragement?

5. Walston satirizes garish imitators of *USA Today*. If a newspaper wants to convert to color, how can it design its own visual identity? How can designers avoid the easiest path, simply copying the splashiest aspects of other papers?

6. Walston describes the color template of *USA Today*'s front page. Do such templates run the risk of degenerating into formulas, or even worse, of pressing the news content into inappropriate forms? How can designers use templates effectively and flexibly at the same time?

7. Walston highlights the trap of the ease of doing graphics in color as opposed to black and white. While color has more resources for conveying information, it also gets out of hand more easily. How can designers keep their "garish" detectors tuned up?

8. Walston says, "We have a color-only theory on page one.... Sometimes we may not have enough photographs in color, so we have developed what we call the 'five-hour news portrait.' On deadline, we will create a picture that may not look exactly like the person in the news, but will be part of a photo illustration that gives you a feeling for the news of the day." Should people in "the truth business" create such approximations just to serve their color formulas?

9. Walston recommends that editors "need to spend a lot of time downstairs in production" to get to know people and procedures. Lately all the experts are advising editors to spend more time on something else. How can busy editors create time to spend elsewhere?

St. Petersburg Times

Michael F. Foley

When I think of color use at the *St. Petersburg Times*, the first word that comes to mind is "experts." Surround yourself with experts. We did. We have some of the best color minds in the business, and the system works. In any situation, you can go ask them, "Can we do this? Can we do it well? How can we do it? Which photo, which illustration is best?" Then you can assume quality control. (You get advice, and you lay off your bet on somebody else: "But he told me we could do this!")

The next word I come up with is "purpose." What are we trying to do? It boils down to basic journalism. We're trying to communicate information to readers. Is it news? Is it late-breaking news? Should we kill the color? That's a question I fear a lot of people don't ask themselves: "Should we kill the color for late-breaking news?"

"Content" is the next word I think of. Is it good? Is it clear? Would you use this picture if it were in black and white? Does it provide a message rather than just enhance the design? These are all tough questions.

Then I think of the word "communication." Communication within the newspaper is extremely important. That's why I ask all these questions. We talk. We involve the people who know. And then we deal with the people who need the information. We talk all the time. We meet in advance of events. We meet during events. We meet after events. We stand around the light table picking the color. The editors are all there. We cooperate. We have a common goal. And then we all decide what to do.

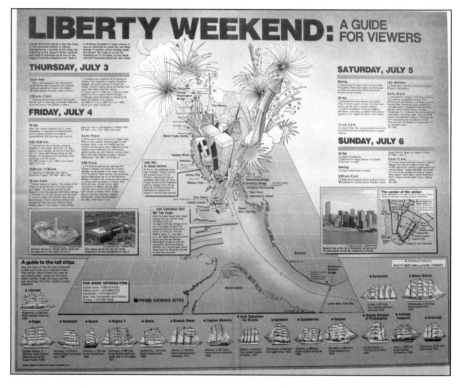

FIG. 3K. Color becomes a dominant element in this double truck entirely devoted to Liberty Weekend. Notice the use of red bars to highlight calendar events. Green dominates the center of the pages, while a layer of brown is used effectively to present a guide to the tall ships. The background of the spread is draped with shades derived from other colors on the page.

FIG. 3L. Compatibility of colors enhances the design of this page. The designer has used a layering system of applying color. Notice the purple leading to the yellow tones as the first color application. White is used for the headline, an effective way to call attention to type.

FIG. 3M. A color photograph, such as this wrap-around photo, can offer that element of surprise that readers always appreciate. The photo was blown up from a 35mm negative, and two screens were used.

There are other words that should not be taken for granted. "Simplicity." "Honesty." Sounds like the Boy Scouts, doesn't it? Obey the law of the pack.

"Commitment." You've heard a lot about that. An important part of commitment is having the best people you can get. It's as simple as that. You've got to have the best people.

Then you must set high standards and stick to them. In short, it's basic journalism. What's the purpose of a newspaper? To report, to explain, to lead, and to entertain.

You must apply these news story guidelines to your art and photos. What's it for, and what's the story? That's a determination for an editor to make, and for all editors to make: the news editor, the art editor, the city editor, the state editor, the photo editor, and probably even the managing editor.

The *Times* has been using color for a long, long time. We used color even before we really had color. On the day of the coldest recorded temperature in Florida, the news editors wanted to illustrate a story about how cold it was. All that was available was black and white. Well, you can change that by running blue ink instead of black. So they printed the entire front page in blue: type, pictures, everything, with a big headline:

BRRRRRRRRRRRRRR
We're Blue! It's Cold!

You may not like that treatment. I didn't. But I didn't have anything to do with it. It was done before I arrived.

Sometimes we choose not to run color. We often make a conscious decision to run black and white. We had a Grand Prix auto race in downtown St. Petersburg last year, and we sent a photographer to get a picture of what the course looked like from the driver's point of view. Naturally we were going to shoot color, but you couldn't see the scene clearly in the color photos. In black and white, you

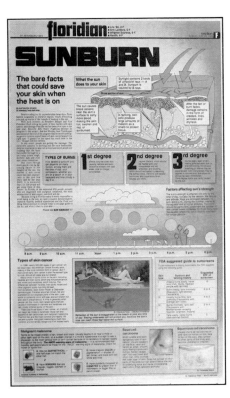

FIG. 3N. The content on this page calls for color conveying the meaning of "sunburn." The layering system "departmentalizes" units on this page. The background has shades of yellow and blue. The art emphasizes red, with the information boxes using various hues of red to give the overall impression of "heat."

could see it better, so we ran the black and white.

Two years ago, we sent a photographer out for Veterans Day shots. You've got the flag, so you've got at least three colors to work with right there. It's hard to do badly. And we got it. But, just as he was leaving the ceremonies, he got a great shot with a camera that had only black and white film in it. What do you think we ran? We also have an afternoon paper, and they ran the color pictures, so it wasn't a waste. But again, we go back to the question of selecting the best picture.

Sometimes you find that color is absolutely necessary for a story or an illustration. For example, without color, it would be difficult to present a

22

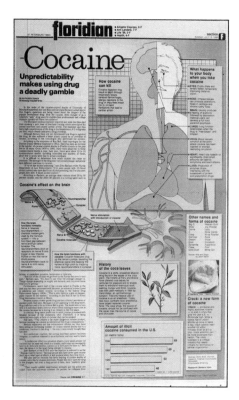

FIG. 3O. This page presents a lot of color without overwhelming the reader, a result of good color coordination. The illustration emphasizes soft earth tones. The type boxes use derivatives of colors in the illustration. No single color dominates this package.

FIG. 3P. Color in maps should follow a consistent style. At the *Times*, all water appears in a certain shade of blue, and land is treated with the darker color edge. Even the type remains consistent. Notice the hues used to frame the maps, ranging from blue to magenta to purple.

FIG. 3Q. White was used as a background for this photo essay page about Jerusalem. The color in the photographs is sufficient to bring impact to the page.

FIG. 3R. Light colors enhance legibility, as in this example in which the top of the page draws on the colors in the illustration for the background. White is used at the bottom of the page, where the bulk of the type appears.

FIG. 3S. The designer and editor worked together on this page to blend the colors, making them more compatible. The two photos in the promos emphasize green and red. The Berlin Wall graphic uses softer shades derived from green and red. Red is picked up at the bottom for the Campaign 86 sig.

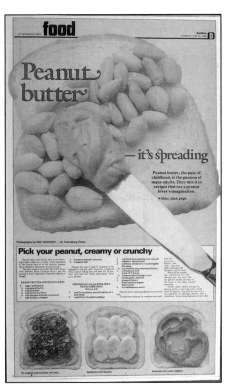

FIG. 3T. The color purple has been used in this Food section front to drape the page, and also for the headline. Since the story concerns peanut butter, the grape jelly justifies the use of purple. Notice how the text on the page appears as part of a separate color layer, a peach tone obtained by mixing yellow and red.

FIG. 3U. This sports segment drapes the box with a soft blue, and green and orange are used for the maps. A neutral peach tone is used for the informational graphic box in the middle, the same color used for the box that becomes the first point of entry into the package at the top.

map showing the different levels of income in various counties of Florida. Food pictures often look yucky in black and white.

So, to use color successfully, go back to the experts. Ask your photographers what works. Praise them when they do well. And encourage them to go out on their own to find good color photos. Our photographers know that if they get a good picture, they can get it printed. That's the kind of encouragement photographers really like, seeing their pictures played very large.

Last year, our very own hurricane hit, and we had all our photographers out. Over the course of five days,

August 31 through September 4, we ran 50 color pictures in the *Times*, and in our afternoon paper, the *Evening Independent*, 12 color pictures. We ran 94 black and white pictures over the same period of time, 15 of those in the *Independent*.

Let's talk about the expense of all this color. Our director of news illustration, George Sweers, put together our color capability, and I give him most of the credit for that, along with Nelson Poynter. What is the ratio of color film shot to color pictures printed? I hesitate to say this, but it's about 100 to one. George admitted that fact to top management during his budget talks, but they still bought

him the film. (He gets just one roll for all of next year!) We spent $24,000 covering one hurricane, not including newsprint.

One more thing I should mention about experts, one thought I would like to leave you with. If you're the expert, be good at it.

By the way, the major reason why my experts are so important to me is that I'm color blind.

Michael F. Foley is managing editor of the St. Petersburg Times, which he joined in 1974 and where he has also served as general assignment reporter, assistant city editor, and metropolitan editor. He is an honor graduate in journalism from the University of Florida.

Questions and Observations

1. Foley's list of words includes the following: "experts, purpose, content, communication, simplicity, honesty," and "commitment." What words would you add to this list of factors for success in color production?

2. Foley says editors must be ready to ask, "Should we kill the color for late-breaking news?" Under what conditions would you recommend this action?

3. Foley says, "The purpose of a newspaper [is] to report, to explain, to lead, and to entertain." Do you agree with these purposes? What others could you add? How can color enhance these purposes in meaningful ways?

4. Foley expresses very basic, old-fashioned, conservative views of news judgment, growing out of a long tradition of print journalism. Can these values survive in a high-tech, highly competitive era dominated by images?

5. Foley recommends "selecting the best picture," regardless of its color or lack of color. Can you envision a day when one of the qualities that makes a picture "the best" will be the simple fact that it is in color? Can you foresee a time when photographers will no longer carry black and white film?

6. Despite the predictions in question five, in budget hearings, how can we justify the high cost of color film and the high ratio of photos shot to photos printed?

N. Christian Anderson

This success story of an individual newspaper could be told by a number of papers. We know that many newspapers in the United States today use color particularly well. *USA Today*, recognized as a newspaper that uses color well, at least uses it widely and reproduces it in a very fine way.

With all due respect to the folks at *USA Today*, I do want to underscore that *USA Today* did not invent color in newspapers. It didn't even perfect it. I'm sure that it has not been perfected. But we should at least give credit to those who have taken color and color reproduction in newspapers to new heights.

USA Today, even with its specific challenge of printing on many different presses and in different locations, has proved that newspapers can reproduce color exceptionally well. That lesson should not be lost on any of us: very simply, if we are willing to make a commitment to do color well, we can do it.

No one would disagree that the *St. Petersburg Times*, under the direction of Bob Haiman, showed the way. There were smaller newspapers that were using color well, but the *Times* showed the way for larger newspapers. They showed not only how to reproduce color very well, but also how to use color very well.

Using color very well depends in part on the content of the photographs being used. Newspapers ought to distinguish themselves, not just by how well they reproduce the color, not just by how much color, but also by what the color says, and by the content of those photographs. Saying that a newspaper does a good job of color encompasses all of these things.

There aren't that many newspapers that do color well. And I'd like to suggest that there are only a few, because only a few are willing to make the commitment.

At the American Newspaper Publishers Association meeting in New

FIG. 3V. This front page shows how the color of the sky was adjusted by the scanner to restore the "true" blue on the day of the Challenger explosion. Other color use on this page is subtle, with a soft peach tone for the promos at the top, effectively picked up for the inside box.

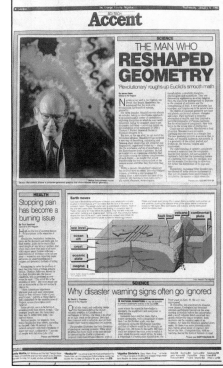

FIG. 3W. The color frames and the background color used for the boxes here unify this page, another example of the important role color can play as a packaging tool. Compatibility and softness of hues are the key to successful color coordination.

Orleans, I gave a talk about what we had done, to an audience mostly of production people. I was delighted to attribute a great part of the success we have had to our production people. They have done such an outstanding job not only of printing color, but also of improving the transparencies that we give them.

I also had to tell them that you simply cannot cost-justify good color. You can't justify it in the normal scheme of things that says, "We'll get a 2.5 year payback on this." Good color has to be done for the long-term benefit of the newspaper, and the publisher has to buy that principle to start with. If the publisher doesn't buy that idea, you can write it off. Some of the production people came up afterwards and said, "You're not living in the real world if you don't cost-justify things." All I wanted to say was: "That's my point. If you don't make that kind of commitment,

you're not going to do color well."

I was also struck by a conversation I overheard at a meeting of editors not too long ago. One said, "Our color isn't worse than anybody else's." That says to me that that newspaper doesn't want to be any better than anybody else. And in a competitive situation, I will guarantee you that excellence makes a difference.

Another editor said, "You guys do color just for color's sake." And I was struck by that particular comment from that particular editor because he works at a newspaper that doesn't do color at all. And I know it's not because that newspaper can't do color; it's unwilling to make the commitment to do color. And that refusal says to me that that paper doesn't want to be better than anybody else.

The Register

I want to talk a little bit about the Orange County *Register*. We have

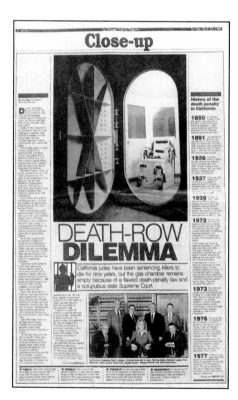

FIG. 3X. This Feature section front makes effective use of color as a unifying element, but leaves the headline in black type, thus making a more powerful statement on the page.

FIG. 3Y. Color photography enhances the design of a page, with very little else needed, as in this example. Quality control makes the difference between good and poor color. Editor Anderson says, "Anyone can do good color if everyone is willing to make a commitment to quality."

FIG. 3Z. A quick color analysis of this page reveals a soft peach background, interrupted only to highlight the text with a white background. The softness of these colors enhances the green in the main illustration. Good color accessorizing requires that designers set priorities.

290,000 circulation, about 26th or 27th in the country in terms of daily circulation. Orange County is the home of Disneyland and the Los Angeles Rams and Knott's Berry Farm and the California Angels. Newport Beach is in Orange County, along with 26 other cities varying in size from 250,000 to 25,000, all told, about 2.1 million residents.

Orange County is south of Los Angeles County and north of San Diego County. It has grown considerably in the past 15 years as companies have moved from Los Angeles and elsewhere into Orange County. A number of relatively large companies have been started from scratch by entrepreneurial men and women who have seen Orange County as a great place to locate.

The economy includes agriculture (although not much citrus anymore), high technology, some manufacturing, and lots and lots of service. Its

people are very well educated and very affluent. The median income of almost $36,000 makes it the 10th most affluent metropolitan area in the country. It's a good place to do business, and a good place for the newspaper business as well. There's lots of advertising.

There are essentially two large newspapers that advertisers choose to use in Orange County, besides four smaller dailies: us and the Orange County edition of the *Los Angeles Times*.

The *Los Angeles Times* is one of the largest newspapers in the country in terms of circulation, and the largest newspaper in the country in terms of advertising lineage. It's been number one in total ad lineage for a number of years. It has more revenue and makes more profit than any other newspaper in the world.

And its newsroom budget was $74 million in 1985.

The Register was sixth in the country in total advertising lineage, full run, in 1984. We were fourth in retail and fifth in classified. And for the first six months of this year, we're still sixth in the country in total lineage, but we've moved up to number three in classified.

Now some people will say that it must be hard to go wrong if you have all of those resources. If you have all that money, you should be able to do well. But just for the record, the 1985 newsroom budget at the Orange County *Register* was 55 percent that of the *St. Petersburg Times*. So we don't have a lot of money to throw around.

The Register is 80 years old this year. It rolled along in what was essentially a suburban area of Los Angeles for about 30 years until the *Los Angeles Times* decided to stake its claim with its Orange County edition in 1968. And the battle was joined. *The Register* then led the *Times* in daily circulation by about 11,500 subscribers, and the *Times* was ahead on Sunday by about 31,000.

FIG. 3AA. A color frame packages three different elements: the map on the upper left, the larger map, and the copy block. Blue is introduced with the promos at the top, then picked up with the rule under the nameplate, and as an accent color in the photograph at the bottom of the page.

FIG. 3BB. The multi-layer approach is used to explain why sunny California is not sunny in June. The first layer is gray, a neutral color that accommodates the second peach tone layer on top. In addition, white highlights a smaller item at the bottom of the page.

28

FIG. 3CC. Green has been used effectively here, inspired by the larger photo, which also yields the soft hue used as a background for the text. In the large photo, the blue from the sky, barely visible through the trees, has been repeated for the initial letter of the text.

FIG. 3DD. The dominance of blue represents a "color attack" approach in this travel page. Notice the use of white as a background for the text blocks. The use of black for the headline introduces the contrast of another color tone.

FIG. 3EE. Even a simple front page like this one can benefit from the use of good color coordination. Notice how the same shade moves the reader from the promos to the photo package, to the bottom right hand corner of the page.

We competed back and forth, and eventually *The Register* led the *Times* in both categories. But by 1979, our daily lead dropped to 38,000, and our Sunday lead was down to 16,000, a loss of 13,000 daily and our Sunday lead cut in half. It was a bad trend. *The Register* at that time produced half of the revenues of Freedom Newspapers Incorporated, and half of the profit. And they did not want to see that situation eroded further by the inroads the *Los Angeles Times* was making.

At that point, the *Times* was very, very strong in advertising generated in Orange County. They had all the department store advertising that emanated from Los Angeles, and we had virtually none. We had a lot of hard goods advertising and a lot of classified, but not much other retail. Then the classifieds started dropping, and that was even worse.

So the owners decided they were going to spend money on the product.

Now coincidentally, the time had come to buy new presses. So they bought two nine-unit Goss Metros with five color half decks. They prepared to print a lot of spot color in the paper because classified advertising, particularly car dealers, demanded a lot of spot color.

Buying those presses was coincidental or an excellent case of timing, depending on your point of view, but coincidental with the fact that they wanted to spend a lot of money on the product. So from 1979 to 1981, the profit margin at *The Register* dropped drastically. And in the five years since then, the profit margin has declined each year by design.

Then the publisher made another decision: he wanted color as good as the *St. Petersburg Times*. He sent people to St. Petersburg to ask how to do it. And they said, "We have a Hell scanner, and we were the first

FIG. 3FF. A color photograph forms the center of visual impact on this front page. The dominant color in the photograph calls attention to the promos above the nameplate, as well as to the illustration accompanying the lead story on the right.

newspaper in the country to have one." So he said, "Well, we have to have one too." He also hired a man from Hell to run it. The publisher told everybody at the newspaper that he wanted color in the paper, and he wanted it done well.

So the presses came on line in late 1979. When I came on board in the fall of 1980, the first deadline color had just been used. The Los Angeles Rams had moved to Anaheim Stadium and opened their exhibition season. We went out there at 6 o'clock at night and took a color picture of the scene for the front page of the next day's paper. And that was the first deadline color *The Register* had published.

But the publisher was not happy about the color situation. He had paid $25 million, and it wasn't happening the way he wanted it. So he called everybody together and said, one more time, that he wanted quality color in the newspaper. He made it clear

that it was the last time he would have to say that, and he looked at me. In the newsroom, we knew that we had to take advantage of the commitment the publisher had made. He was serious about it, and we had to be too.

Now here's where our story gets a little bit different. Not only did he tell us he wanted the best color in the country, he also decided that we should not worry about how much it cost from a production standpoint. So he said there would be no cost accounting in any way, shape, or form for color. No worry about how much we spent for ink. No worry about how much we spent in other aspects of producing color. And to this day that practice holds true.

All of this was a tall order back in 1980. It was particularly tough on our photo staff, which numbered seven when I arrived, none of whom had ever shot color for a newspaper. We hired an eighth photographer a couple of months later, and she hadn't shot color for a newspaper either. There were some further philosophical differences between me and some of the photo staff. Some of them felt that it was better to do certain photographs in black and white because they would capture the mood of that particular situation better than color would. We don't have those philosophical differences any longer.

We hired a new director of photography and a new assistant managing editor for graphics, and then the fun began. We in the newsroom ordained, as the publisher had ordained, that we would do color well. That meant that we would shoot photo assignments simply for their content value, for their news value, and we would do so in color. No assignment would be made for its color quality, and no story would get different play because it had a color photograph to go along with it.

Obviously there was a steep learning curve. Among other things, we learned how to dupe color to black and white. We worked hard at it. And

we had a lot of sessions with our staff, an in-house training program. We brought in people to explain how to do lighting. We taught them that what looks nice on screens doesn't necessarily look nice in newspapers, particularly on newsprint of the quality that most of us have. We had a scanner operator who screamed, sometimes in German, whenever a transparency wasn't absolutely perfect, and we had to go through a real educational process with him. We would say, "Well, gee, we didn't get this right; but then you can't always have the best light when you're out shooting a news assignment." And he kept objecting. He even had names for a couple of the photographers; one of them was "The Prince of Darkness." With that kind of cooperation, we were having a great time!

All of this was before the Chromacom came along. However, the operator was able to manipulate the scanner to correct some of the color shift problems we had. And that helped us a great deal. The press operators were absolutely terrific, although we did have a problem there too. We had to replace one press superintendent because the presses were not being kept clean. And that made a world of difference as well.

Once that problem was licked, the press operators were excited about how well they could print color. Then it was much up to the newsroom to do its thing. Good color is not just good reproduction, but also using color particularly well. So we made it very clear to the editors at *The Register* that color was a key part of our personality.

We knew we had a competitive advantage. The *Los Angeles Times* could not print color in all its editions, because it was still converting from letterpress to offset in its presses downtown and in some of the early presses in Orange County as well. So we knew that we could distinguish ourselves from our primary competitor by using a lot of color and using it well.

The newsroom has color. Every section front, every position that is available, when it wants it, as long as there is press capacity. And although it's a good problem to have, unfortunately advertising sometimes pushes us out of color availability on all section fronts.

Good color is deceptively easy if you are willing to make the commitment, but that is what it takes. First of all, it takes leadership. I am a firm believer that publishers can ordain good color. And it takes people who believe in that leadership, and who have the talent and enthusiasm to make it happen.

Mediocrity, on the other hand, is very easy to accomplish, because it doesn't take much effort at all. Excellence takes effort and patience. Good color doesn't happen overnight. We made mistakes along the way, and

we still do. We don't always give the color lab great transparencies. We don't always get the presses started on time. And we don't always get the paper delivered to everybody who wants to get it.

We do know a few things from our particular experience. First of all, you have to have the right equipment. But more importantly, you have to have the right people. Finally, any success that we've had can be summed up in just a simple sentence: professionalism is painstaking attention to detail. If we all live by that thought, I think we all can be successful.

N. Christian Anderson is editor of the Orange County Register, which won the Pulitzer Prize for spot news photography in 1985. Mr. Anderson was managing editor of The Seattle Times before joining The Register in 1980, where he supervises a staff of 260, producing a newspaper considered as one of the most innovative in color use in the U.S.

FIG 3GG. Color photography dominates the cover page of this special supplement devoted to the Olympics. Notice the background color used to package the entire unit, a peach tone derived from a magenta and yellow combination.

FIG. 3HH. When color photographs are the dominant design element, as in this section front, the designer does not emphasize much spot color elsewhere. This page would carry less visual impact if the index column on the left had color numbers and symbols. In this case, less is more.

Questions and Observations

1. All three of the papers reporting here stress commitment as the key to printing excellent color. Think about all the meanings of commitment in this context, especially about the various levels at which these commitments must operate.

2. Anderson distinguishes between "reproducing" color very well and "using" it very well. How can this distinction guide discussions between production and editorial staffs in planning color capability?

3. Anderson believes "that you simply cannot cost-justify good color.... Good color has to be done for the long-term benefit of the newspaper, and the publisher has to buy that principle to start with." In these cost-conscious times, focusing mostly on short-term gains, how can we convince ourselves and our publishers to make the expensive long-term commitment to printing quality color? Write down a list of arguments and factors you might use.

4. Anderson also believes that "in a competitive situation,...excellence makes a difference." Should that belief be the first item on your list in question three?

5. Anderson quotes another editor, who said, "You guys do color just for color's sake." How can we distinguish between merely faddish color and color employed for journalistic and business purposes?

6. Anderson says his publisher told him to print quality color with "no cost accounting in any way, shape, or form." First of all, do you believe him? Second, can stories of such apparent fiscal recklessness damage arguments for starting up quality color? Maybe we should just attribute such tales to Southern California exuberance.

7. Both Foley and Anderson stress the retraining of photographers. Consider the difficulties of recasting their craft against a long tradition of black-and-white photojournalism. Maybe that tradition gets in the way of retraining editors too.

8. Anderson describes a difficult period of retraining, new equipment, perilous finances, and rethinking as fun and exciting. We tend to forget the thrills when we forecast all that has to be done to start up new enterprises, especially one so complex as color capability.

9. Anderson says, "We knew that we could distinguish ourselves from our primary competitor by using a lot of color and using it well." Just "using a lot of color" will not provide that competitive edge, but also "using it well."

10. Anderson closes with this thought: "Professionalism is painstaking attention to detail." How can managers, who concentrate on the long and large view, achieve such attention to detail, both for themselves and in their staffs?

4 Poynter Research Findings

Mario R. Garcia
Robert Bohle

Newspapers are using more color today. Oddly enough, four of the largest dailies (the *Los Angeles Times*, the *New York Daily News*, *The New York Times*, and *The Wall Street Journal*) use no color at all in their news sections. But beyond this conservative group, we'd be surprised to find many daily papers not using at least spot color regularly.

Between 1979 and 1983, the number of newspapers using color more than doubled, from 12 percent to 28 percent. Fifty-three percent of all weekday papers had color in 1983. In a survey of papers with circulation under 75,000, 66 percent used color regularly, and another 18 percent used it occasionally.

Although statistics cannot describe the *quality* of use, clearly much color use is uninformed. It lacks purpose, is not used journalistically, and is usually not used functionally. Often color seems an aimless vagrant on the page, utilized not as a design tool, but as something added simply because it is available.

The push for color in newspapers seems to have outdistanced the ability to use it well. And those in a position to determine how color is used are often asked many questions for which they have no good answers. The idea of a Poynter Institute Color Symposium coupled with an original research project originated as an attempt to answer some of these questions, to articulate intelligently both data and advice that editors could use to make decisions about color in their newspapers.

The most important initial question was: "What questions need to be asked?"

Initial Questionnaire

Editors, designers, and professionals in the printing business were sent a questionnaire in January 1985, asking them a number of questions about newspaper color. The survey asked what they would like to see researched and discussed at a symposium.

The respondents rated the use of color in American newspapers at 4.2 on a 1-to-10 scale, or less than mediocre. The scores ranged from a one to a seven.

When asked to name the papers that used color well and those that used it poorly, respondents tended to agree. Oddly enough, some newspapers, including *USA Today*, the *St. Petersburg Times*, the Orange County *Register*, and the *Chicago Tribune*, among others, made BOTH lists. This paradox shows that even experts may not agree on the definition of "good" use of color.

When asked what characterized good color use, respondents pointed to the following practices:

• functional, not decorative, use of color;

• clean spot color;

• harmonious tones based on sound color choices;

• quality control that leads to good reproduction;

• good photo content;

• effective layout and design to accommodate the color choices.

FIG. 4A. One of the participants in the color research project looks at a front page of *The Daily Times*, the prototype newspaper, and records her impressions on the questionnaire during the eye movement segment of the test in Richmond.

The characteristics of "bad" color cited are:

• non-functional use;

• dark tints, resulting from poor or no quality control;

• poor color combinations, the mixing of incompatible tones;

• colors inappropriate to the subjects of graphics.

Review of the Literature

While these results were being tallied, we began a search for previous studies about color, especially about color in newspapers. Although this symposium celebrated 25 years of regular color use in newspapers, we found few studies about newspaper color, underlining the need for more research in the area.

Before discussing the methods and the results of the subsequent research project, we wish to outline the results of the search for information. The research surveyed falls into six categories: reader preferences, advertising analogies, symbolism, physiological effects, personality attributes, and psychological factors.

Most of the research about color itself has marginal interest for newspaper journalists: the physics and optics of color, colors in fashion and interior design, etc.

Reader Preferences

The most interesting research specifically about newspaper design and color has been done by J. W. Click and G. H. Stempel, who have studied reader reaction to page design several times. Their 1976 study found that readers highly preferred pages with color halftones over pages with black-and-white halftones. A later study found that readers prefer modular pages with color to traditional pages without color.

The only research we found that had anything to do with newspaper spot color concerned the background color on a tabloid insert aimed at architects (Donath, 1984). Red had a much higher attraction rating than any other color. The other colors tested (yellow, brown, blue, and green) were rated nearly the same. Bright yellow scored better than muted yellow, but muted green was better than bright green. No difference was found in the reds and blues.

In Ruth Clark's study, *Relating to Readers in the '80s*, readers were asked to respond to the following statement: "I wish newspapers would use more color and color pictures." Surprisingly, only 46 percent agreed, although agreement was higher for the 18-to-24 age group (52 percent), minorities (52 percent), and non-readers (61 percent).

An International Newspaper Advertising and Marketing Executives (INAME) survey found that readers see newspapers with ROP (Run of the Press) color as "progressive." The study also noted that readers think color photos are more realistic than black-and-white ones, that readers dislike poor color reproduction, and that color use may boost readership (English, 1985).

Advertising Research

Much of the media color research has been done by advertisers or groups interested in advertising. Because readers perceive color the same way in an ad or in editorial content, we can learn a lot from these studies.

In ads, studies have shown that color *generally* pulls more reader attention. Also, the more color surrounding an element, the less power that element has to attract.

Other results include:

• On 9 of 11 ad pairs in color versus black and white, the color version was remembered better. Color ads with lots of color surrounding them were weaker against black and white.

• Color is more important than illustration in gaining attention.

• In a study of color and store design, red tended to attract the most attention, but its active nature made people tenser than did other colors.

• In a Newspaper Advertising Bureau study, body type in a color ad was read by 80 percent of subjects; in a black-and-white ad, only 50 percent read it.

• In a test of *recall* as opposed to attention, a color ad was recalled more frequently. But the black-and-white ad beat color in depth of recall, that is, in how much the subjects remembered about the ad.

• In a study of a long-term ad campaign, black and white did better on recall than did color.

From these results, we could say that color works better for the fast grab, for the quick emotional appeal, but that black and white produces a better response where more in-depth thinking is desired.

Manufacturers are also interested in the effects of color characteristics of their products. Black, red, purple, and blue are seen as "heavy" colors; yellow, orange, white, and pastels as

FIG. 4B. (Page C) Nearly all the subjects entered this page above the fold. Usually the main photo and the main story were the first and second stopping points, supporting the accepted theories of attraction and eye movement on a newspaper page.

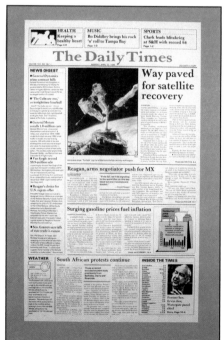

FIG. 4C. (Page G) The simple addition of color to the nameplate type did little to alter eye movement on the page. The black-and-white promo boxes still got little eye traffic.

FIG. 4D. (Page K) Putting a color photo below the fold on an otherwise black-and-white page creates a powerful visual magnet. Even in the classic "Terminal Optical Area" on the page, the element was seen first by approximately one-quarter of the subjects.

"light" colors. Thus, potential customers may perceive a red or dark blue vacuum cleaner as heavy and difficult to work with.

Symbolism

The eye can see several million colors, but we have names for very few of them. In fact, the basic color vocabulary has only about a dozen words. Other words for colors are:

- Qualifiers (light or dark).
- The name of something else (gold or lemon or puce, which comes from the Latin word for flea, *pulex*. Yes, fleas have puce-colored bellies.)
- The joining of two colors (blue-green, red-orange).
- Whimsical coinages (magenta, a dye created in 1859, was named after the recent Battle of Magenta in Northern Italy).

Color by itself conveys meaning. In almost any culture, in almost any period of man's development, red has meant danger. It was found to be the third color word added to a "primitive" culture's vocabulary (after black and white) in nearly all of 2,000 cultures studied. But different cultures have different color symbols. In the West, black is the color of mourning and funerals; in China, it is white. Eskimos have no word for brown in their vocabulary, but they have many words for different shades of white.

Physiological Effects

So, to a certain extent, color has cultural shadings. But studies have also shown that reactions to certain colors (red, for instance) are similar. The wavelength of red, an active color, actually excites brain waves. Thus, regardless of cultural background, someone seeing the color red has certain physiological reactions.

Red has been found in several studies to raise the respiration rate, blood pressure, and the number of eye blinks per minute. Blue, on the other hand, was found to lower all three.

Time spent before a red screen was estimated as shorter than the same amount of time spent before a blue screen in one test. Thus, red, the "active" color, perhaps made the subject feel "busier," so time went faster. Blue, the "passive" color, calmed the subjects so much that time seemed to lag.

Another study found that the warm colors have a strong excitation effect and may cause problems in concentrating on a task. Another test found reaction times 12 percent higher than normal under a red light. A green light actually slowed responses.

Red has been found to be more arousing than green, as is violet. Perhaps the ends of the spectrum (red and violet) may be more arousing than the center (green).

FIG. 4E. (Page S) This page contains similarly colored elements and color photos. The addition of this much color drastically changed where many subjects entered the page and where their eyes traveled next. The similarity of the color tint blocks may cause the reader to try to make content connections as well.

FIG. 4F. (Page Y) This so-called "Carmen Miranda" page caused some confusion among readers as to the proper starting point. The variety of starting points and eye travel paths on this page was greater than on any other.

Personality Attributes

Several researchers have tried to attach personality attributes to color preferences. Faber Birren, a leading authority on color and the author of many books on the subject, said that red is preferred by active people, orange by friendly, yellow by the high-minded, and blue-green by the fastidious.

Blue is most often cited as a favorite color, with red second. In fact, the ends of the color spectrum, where apparently more arousal strength exists, seem to be preferred in general over the middle (green). *USA Today*, after extensive research, perhaps playing to the public's favorite color, chose a distinctive blue nameplate.

Birren also found that Latins tended to prefer reds and oranges, while Scandinavians prefer blues and greens. He also postulated that red is better for emotionally determined actions, while green is better when the goal is exact fulfillment of a task.

Psychological Factors

Many color psychologists believe that people are either warm-color dominant or cool-color dominant, and that these general color preferences are tied to many other personality traits. E. R. Jaensch associates warm colors with the "primitive" responses of children: excitation and extroversion. Warm colors tend to be preferred by brunets, he says. On the other hand, cool colors, preferred by blonds, go with more mature responses and introversion.

Other psychological associations are commonly attached to certain colors:

RED: passionate, exciting, enraged, fierce, intense.

ORANGE: jovial, energetic, hilarious, exuberant, forceful.
YELLOW: cheerful, inspiring, high spirited, celestial, healthy.
GREEN: peaceful, refreshing, quieting, ghastly, terrifying, guilty.
BLUE: subduing, melancholy, sober, gloomy, furtive, fearful.
PURPLE: mournful, dignified, mystic, lonely, desperate.
WHITE: pure, clean, frank, youthful, normal.
BLACK: depressed, funereal, dispirited, dead.

Young children generally prefer bright, fully saturated colors. Teenagers and adults tend to prefer pastels. Researchers disagree on the existence of color preference by sex. Among college students tested in one study, those who preferred warm colors had quicker reaction times, scored higher on a "heterosexuality" scale, and rated erotic jokes higher on an evaluation test than did those who preferred cool colors.

Robert Chestnut of the Ted Bates Agency in New York points out that individual color preferences change over the course of a single day for no apparent reason. So asking readers what color they would prefer on your nameplate may well be a waste of time.

Many of the studies referred to and listed in the bibliography have been severely criticized. In fact, we have to say that we know very little for certain about how people react to color.

Despite high interest in color in the newspaper industry, not much public research had been done. Some proprietary research, such as that done by *USA Today* before its launch, is not available.

The New Research

Respondents to The Poynter Institute survey about color had numerous questions about color they would like answered, but not all questions could be answered by one research project. With that limitation in mind, our

project attempted to discover how color affects eye movement on a page, to replicate the earlier Click and Stempel methodology, and to sample general reader opinions about color in newspapers.

The Prototype Newspapers

We decided against using slides to present the test pages to the subjects, preferring instead real pages. Readers could then respond to more normal conditions, the first color test ever done in this way. Previous studies had used papers from different cities, thus losing the ability to control other variables.

We wanted to keep everything on the pages exactly the same, except for color. If differing opinions surfaced about the pages, we could be more certain that the differences occurred because of color and not some other

FIG. 4G. (Page B) The photos on this page drew all the attention. After visiting the main photo of the bear, most subjects looked next at the secondary photo. As on the front pages, the promos in black and white drew little traffic.

reason, such as the nature of the stories or the size of the headlines.

The front pages differ in one respect: on some pages the "Inside" box in the lower right-hand corner has a one-column, black-and-white mug shot of former Sen. Sam Ervin; on others, the box is a column wider and carries a larger color halftone of a woman and an animal.

The *St. Petersburg Times* agreed to put together the pages and print enough copies for the four test sites. Pegie Stark and Dave Rettig of the *Times* designed a front page, a life-styles front, and a sports front for a fictitious newspaper called *The Daily Times.* A black-and-white version of each page was printed, as well as pages with a wide variety of color treatments, including color half-tones, promos, informational graphics, flags, and tint blocks over type.

The Subjects

We conducted the tests in four cities: Richmond, Va., Springfield, Mo., Fresno, Cal., and St. Petersburg, Fla. We selected these sites because they offered a wide variety of demo-graphics in their readers and a variety of color usage by the papers. The newspapers in the test cities selected the 83 subjects. Generally, they were selected to represent a wide variety of demographic variables, and not to represent overall newspaper readership (Table 1). Most (78 percent) read a paper five or more times per week, and 95 percent read a newspaper at least three times a week.

The subjects compared favorably with the "average" newspaper reader except for education: the group proved much more educated than the average. Although we have drawn some tentative conclusions from our

Demographics
Based on subject sample at four test sites.

SEX	Male	49%
	Female	51%
AGE	18 to 34	34%
	35 to 44	20%
	45 to 54	13%
	55 to 64	13%
	65 plus	20%
RACE	Caucasian	66%
	Black	22%
	Hispanic	12%
EDUCATION	High school or less	17%
	Some college or tech school	37%
	College degree	46%
INCOME	Under $15,000	25%
	$15,000-25,000	29%
	$25,000-35,000	29%
	Above $35,000	17%
MEDIA USE	Read a paper at least 3 days per week	95%
	Read a paper at least 5 days per week	78%
COLOR PREFERENCE	Blue	61%
	Red	18%
	Yellow	8%
	Green	7%
	Purple	3%
	Orange	1%

TABLE 1

FIG. 4H. (Page E) Adding only spot color drastically changed the way subjects looked at the page. They still entered at the main photo, but after that, most saw the headline, now in blue, and then skipped past the photo to the tint block at the bottom of the page.

FIG. 4I. (Page F) The bear in full color is a much stronger image, and the attraction scores reflected that. The eye movement on this page did not change much from the spot page except that nearly everyone saw the bear first.

FIG. 4J. (Page V) This black-and-white page is attractive, with a strong photo above the fold balanced against a screened football schedule graphic. Nevertheless, on this page, subjects preferred to look at the photographs first, starting as always with the main photo.

Eye Movement

Adjusted percentage of page element selected most often for seen first, second, third.

FRONT PAGES

Page	Seen First	Seen Second	Seen Third
C	Top photo 53%	Top story 26%	Digest & TS 17%
S	Top photo 51%	Top photo 26%	Index 26%
Y	Top photo 43%	Top story 19%	Digest & Index 21%
K	Top photo 34%	Top photo 30%	Index 21%
G	Top photo 54%	Top story 27%	Top story 18%

LIFESTYLE FRONTS

Page	Seen First	Seen Second	Seen Third
B	Top photo 51%	Second photo 25%	Second photo 27%
E	Top photo 47%	Main head 19%	People box 28%
F	Top photo 70%	Main head 29%	People box 30%

SPORTS FRONTS

Page	Seen First	Seen Second	Seen Third
V	Top photo 40%	Top photo 29%	Second photo 17%
W	Top photo 24%	Top photo 24%	Digest 18%
H	Top photo 64%	Top photo, flag 19%	Top story 18%

TABLE 2

Visual Magnetism Index

Index is the sum of multiplying "seen first" adjusted percentage by 3, "seen second" by 2, and "seen third" by 1.

FRONT PAGES

Page	Element	Index
C	Top photo	197
	Top story	99
	Promos	37
S	Top photo	205
	Index	107
	Promos	43
Y	Top photo	167
	Index	57
	Digest	51
K	Top photo	162
	Index	126
	Top story	37
G	Top photo	182
	Top story	72
	Digest	42

LIFESTYLE FRONTS

Page	Element	Index
B	Top photo	201
	Main head	136
	Second photo	77
E	Top photo	171
	Main head	158
	Second photo	67
F	Top photo	240
	Main head	112
	Second photo	73

SPORTS FRONTS

Page	Element	Index
V	Top photo	178
	Top story	95
	Flag	75
W	Top photo	120
	Flag	89
	Info graphic	75
H	Top photo	230
	Top story	51
	Flag	46
	2nd photo	45

TABLE 3

pilot study, care should be taken before generalizing to a larger population with much certainty.

Eye Movement

For the eye movement test, a trained interviewer showed subjects one test page at a time. All tests were conducted one-on-one. After the readers saw the page for a few seconds, they were asked where their eye "first fell." This terminology was used instead of "where did you look" or "what did you see," because these terms imply volition, something we wanted to rule out.

Readers were told before the tests that content was not necessarily important, and that we were interested in their reactions toward how the

FIG. 4K. (Page W) The main photo drew much less initial attention on this page, in part because of the addition of color. The schedule, now in color, had much more pull than it did in black and white.

FIG. 4L. (Page H) The main photo in color is a much more powerful visual magnet. The flag also received a lot of attention, perhaps because the dominant blue of the photo is reflected in the word "Sports."

FIG. 4M. (Page C) Overall, the black-and-white front was the least liked of the five pages tested for reader opinion. Many subjects found the page more difficult, as well as somewhat less important and believable. The page was also described as the least loud and modern.

page *looked*. We first tabulated the results by rating how frequently each element on the page was cited for each of the three questions: Where did your eye first fall? Next? After that? (Table 2). But, because in some cases a single element finished first *and* second on a page, it was difficult to see the relative strengths of the elements.

So we created a "Visual Magnetism Index" for each element on the page (Table 3). Essentially, the "seen first" responses by each subject earned three points, the "seen next" responses two, and the "after that" responses one. The responses were summed to create the index.

Color Attracts

Color clearly made a difference in eye movement, even though the main photo on all the pages drew the most attention. In fact, the placement and size of the main photo surpassed all other factors.

On the front pages, after first visiting the main photo, readers usually were attracted to the color on the page, process or spot, even if that movement meant going below the fold. On the black-and-white page and on the page with only a color nameplate, the first move was generally from the photo to the lead story.

When color was added below the fold, the eye was often drawn there after the main photo. In a sense then, color could be seen as keeping the reader from getting right to the news.

On the lifestyle pages, color played an even more interesting role. Despite the obvious strong attraction of photos, a blue tint block over type at the bottom of the page was able to move many eyes past a three-column by three-inch photo.

The all black-and-white page showed high eye traffic on the two photos. The pages with color, even the page with only spot color, showed the ability of spot color, no matter where it was used, to attract the eye.

The three sports pages followed the same pattern: photos were the big draw on the black-and-white page. A gray-screened football schedule was *not* enough to draw the eye below the fold, whereas one in color was.

Finally, the sports flag drew a lot of reader attention, but this pattern was not true on either the fronts or the lifestyle pages. Two of the sports flags appeared in spot blue, but even the flag on the all black-and-white page received heavy eye traffic: 25 percent stopped there first.

This anomaly may be explained by the fact that the main photo on the sports pages, a picture of pro golfer Judy Clark bent over a putt, did not have the attraction of a space shot on page one or a bear on the lifestyle pages, so readers stopped elsewhere. Also, the additional white space around the short word "sports" may have added to the attraction.

FIG. 4N. (Page A) Even the addition of a red *"Daily Times"* in the nameplate seemed to improve opinions about the paper. This page outperformed the heavily pink page in believability.

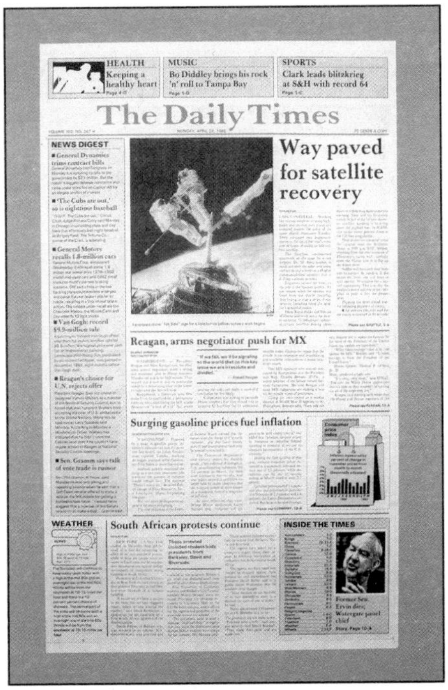

FIG. 4O. (Page M) Reassuringly, this page was rated much louder than the spot blue page, underlining the activity of red for subjects, and the relative passivity of blue. For some reason, the page's worst performance was in believability.

Reader Opinions

We know that typography and format variables (as well as content) affect how people think about a newspaper. As part of this study, The Poynter Institute wanted to discover how color use in a paper affected reader opinions about the paper as a whole.

We decided to study reader opinions two ways: (1) by using a set of 20 word-pair scales that have been used in previous studies, and (2) by using a series of pairs of pages and forcing subjects to choose one over the other on the basis of an evaluative word.

Semantic Differentials

For this test, readers were given a page, and asked to pay no particular attention to the content. They had to rate it on each of the 20 word-pair scales on a 1-to-7 scale. The subjects saw five pages, varying from totally black and white to full color: all black and white, all black and white except a spot red nameplate, black-and-white halftones with blue spot color, black-and-white halftones with spot red, and the so-called "Carmen Miranda" page with a main color graphic, a color halftone, and multiple spot colors. The order of the pages and the order of the word pairs varied at all four test sites.

The 20 word pairs were divided into five general "factors":

Evaluative: pleasant/unpleasant, valuable/worthless, important/unimportant, interesting/boring.

Ethical: fair/unfair, truthful/untruthful, responsible/irresponsible, biased/unbiased, accurate/inaccurate.

Stylistic: exciting/dull, fresh/stale, easy/difficult, neat/messy, colorful/colorless.

Potency: bold/timid, loud/soft, powerful/weak.

Activity: tense/relaxed, modern/old-fashioned, active/passive.

The major concern was whether use of color would negatively affect the serious tone of the delivery of important news, that is, how would color affect ratings of importance or ac-

curacy? We also predicted that the more colorful pages would score high in the stylistic and activity factors. All 10 possible pairs of the five pages were tested for significant differences on each word pair.

Results

Readers clearly like color (Table 4). More importantly, the use of color did not reduce estimations of the ethical nature of the newspaper.

There were no statistically significant differences among any possible page pairs on four of the five ethical factors. On the fifth, "fair/unfair," the only significant difference was between the full-color page (mean equals 5.10) and the all black-and-white page (4.75). The difference, however, is slight and significant at a fairly low level when compared with the other results. Generally then, color did not affect how readers rated the paper on ethical factors.

There were also no significant dif-

ferences between any pair on "neat/messy" and "relaxed/tense," something of a surprise.

On four of the word pairs (important/unimportant, easy/difficult, valuable/worthless, and loud/soft), the differences proved so slight as to lack any significance. Leaving out the full-color page in these calculations showed almost no significant differences. Thus, the use of one spot color, even a heavy use, may not change reader opinions in these areas, compared with a black-and-white page.

There were large and highly significant differences between nearly all page pairs on the nine remaining word-pairs. Most of these, however, are expected differences on stylistic or activity word-pairs on which color would naturally make a difference. The large differences here were reassuring from a validity standpoint.

On "colorful/colorless, modern/old-fashioned, active/passive," and

FIG. 4P. (Page L) Besides being seen as less loud than the pink one, this page rated higher on the believability scale than even the much-favored full-color "Carmen Miranda" page. The page also rated well on "easy."

FIG. 4Q. (Page R) The fact that this page was rated so highly by the subjects might be an artifact of the method. The higher color content of the page may have induced the subject to rate the evaluation word as more powerful. We need further study before deciding that readers like this use of color.

"fresh/stale," the differences were large, and in the direction expected. The remaining results, however, provide more interesting insights into how readers perceive color in newspapers.

The full-color page was seen as more interesting than the black-and-white page by a full two points (on a seven-point scale), an astounding difference on a scale that size. A half-point difference is often considered significant. The spot color pages beat the black-and-white page by a full point, also a very large separation. Clearly, color interests readers.

The same basic story was true on "pleasant/unpleasant": color soundly whipped the black-and-white page. The black-and-white page also was a big loser to color use of any kind on three other pairs: "Exciting/dull, powerful/weak," and "bold/timid."

Paired Comparisons

On this test, one word from a word pair from each of the five factor groups was selected and presented to the subjects one at a time. Considering each of the five words in turn, readers were presented with the 10 possible pairs of pages and asked to select one as having "more" of whatever word they were presented with.

For instance, using "importance" as the evaluative word, subjects were presented with the 10 possible pairs of pages, each time being asked which one of the two pages seemed "more important."

Results

In general, this method supported the results of the semantic differential test (Table 5). On "modern," as expected, the full-color page was a big winner over all the pages, especially the black-and-white page. Also, on "loud," the same order of preference of pages and the same large differences were found. The spot red page was seen as much "louder" than the spot blue page, something one would expect from "active" red and "passive" blue.

With "easy," the differences a-

mong the pages decreased. In other words, the readers found it more difficult to choose one page over another. The full-color page was still seen as easiest, and spot blue was easier than spot red, and the black-and-white page was seen as the most "difficult" page.

On the words in the evaluative category ("important") and the ethical one ("believable," a slight change from the word pairs) respectively, the differences proved even less. The full-color page remained most "important," but the black-and-white page moved significantly higher. Spot blue was seen as slightly more "important" than spot red.

On "believable," the pages were rated very close together. Again, this finding means that, overall, subjects found it very difficult to choose one page as more "believable" than another, based on color. The full-color page totally lost its edge. Spot blue scored higher (59 to 56), though the difference is not large enough to claim much more than a tie. Perhaps more interestingly, the spot red page fell below the page printed in all black and white with a red nameplate (51 to 45).

Paired Comparisons

Adjusted percentages selecting each page in pair.

Pages	Important	Easy	Believable	Modern	Loud
A	70.9	72.2	67.1	83.5	88.6
C	29.1	27.8	32.9	16.5	11.4
A	36.7	26.6	39.2	14.1	38.0
L	63.3	73.4	60.8	85.9	62.0
A	36.7	27.8	49.4	7.6	10.1
M	63.3	72.2	50.6	92.4	89.9
A	32.9	24.1	43.0	5.1	11.4
R	67.1	75.9	57.0	94.9	88.6
C	25.3	12.7	30.4	5.1	12.7
L	74.7	87.3	69.6	94.9	87.3
C	32.9	21.5	45.6	10.1	8.9
M	67.1	78.5	54.4	89.9	91.1
C	34.2	24.1	41.8	5.1	7.6
R	65.8	75.9	58.2	94.9	92.4
L	60.3	57.0	68.4	46.2	17.7
M	39.7	43.0	31.6	53.8	82.3
L	36.7	32.9	46.8	8.9	7.6
R	63.3	67.1	53.2	91.1	92.4
M	29.1	29.1	39.2	12.7	13.9
R	70.9	70.9	60.8	87.3	86.1

Adjusted relative index (scale of 0-100):

Important:	R (64)	L (57)	M (51)	A (47)	C (35)
Believable:	L (59)	R (56)	A (51)	M (45)	C (40)
Easy:	R (68)	L (62)	M (55)	A (41)	C (26)
Loud:	R (85)	M (69)	L (44)	A (37)	C (15)
Modern:	R (87)	M (63)	L (60)	A (26)	C (13)

TABLE 5

Semantic differentials

A 1-to-7 scale was used. Figures are mean scores for each word pair. Word listed first was at low end of scale.

Word Pair	Page M	L	R	A	C
EVALUATIVE					
Unimportant/Important	5.08	4.96	5.45	4.95	4.81
Worthless/Valuable	4.71	4.51	4.88	4.74	4.41
Boring/Interesting	4.61	4.71	5.71	4.34	3.73
Unpleasant/Pleasant	4.88	4.85	5.46	4.46	4.02
ETHICAL					
Inaccurate/Accurate	4.98	4.93	5.17	5.08	5.04
Irresponsible/Responsible	5.04	5.22	5.23	5.16	4.96
Untruthful/Truthful	5.06	5.06	5.07	5.00	5.11
Unfair/Fair	4.96	4.93	5.10	4.98	4.75
Biased/Unbiased	4.28	4.41	4.33	4.40	4.17
STYLISTIC					
Difficult/Easy	4.55	4.89	5.08	4.44	4.25
Stale/Fresh	4.69	4.76	5.61	4.23	3.83
Messy/Neat	4.88	4.66	4.83	4.79	4.39
Colorless/Colorful	4.43	4.66	6.48	3.53	2.35
Dull/Exciting	4.51	4.29	5.58	3.92	3.37
POTENCY					
Soft/Loud	3.81	3.82	5.52	3.69	3.58
Weak/Powerful	4.53	4.47	5.37	4.23	3.85
Timid/Bold	4.45	4.58	5.90	4.22	3.83
ACTIVITY					
Tense/Relaxed	4.14	4.35	4.12	4.24	4.14
Passive/Active	4.51	4.69	5.88	4.20	3.52
Old fashioned/Modern	5.08	5.01	6.10	4.17	3.43
MEAN	4.66	4.69	5.34	4.44	4.08

TABLE 4

Comparing the two spot color pages, exactly alike except for the color, yields intriguing results. The spot red page was seen as "louder" (the obvious result) and more "modern." But the spot blue was found "easier," slightly more "important," and much more "believable." This difference suggest opportunities for future study.

Demographics

Although the study was not meant to be generalized to the entire newspaper audience, the subject demographic data were analyzed to see if any differences in response could be tied to age, sex, race, education, income, city of residence, or media use.

Few significant differences were found in any of these areas. The few differences showed no apparent pattern of response. And we predict that a larger, more representative sample would respond in much the same way. A few of the more interesting tendencies in the data follow:

• The more education the subjects had, the less enamored they seemed with color. For instance, on the evaluative or ethical factors, the more educated tended to prefer black and white over the pages with color. We should probably interpret this finding in conjunction with the fact that the less-educated also tended to rate the color pages as "easier" than the black and white.

• The subjects in the markets with heavier use of color (Springfield and St. Petersburg) seem to like color better than did the subjects in the other two markets. For instance, the color pages did better on "believable" on the paired comparison test in the color cities than in Richmond and Fresno.

• Older subjects seemed to like color better than did younger subjects. This finding seems to contradict the results of the Clark study, which said that the desired 18-to-34 age group would prefer more color in newspapers. One reason may be that older readers may find color helpful because it helps to organize the page, that is, tint blocks over type show the beginning and end of a story more clearly. In our study, older subjects tended to rate the color pages as "easier" than the black-and-white pages.

Color and Initial Attraction

Although in most cases the subjects' eyes first fell on the main photo on the page (color or black and white), our research found color to be a strong influence on eye movement. Color affects initial attraction to a page, as well as where the eye moves from that point.

The Power of Color

Despite the overwhelming attraction of the main photo, color on the page diminished that power. Color was sometimes more powerful than black-and-white photos in moving the eye after initial entry to the page. In some cases, a color tint block over type had enough attraction to move a reader past a secondary photograph. A gray screen over type does not seem to have the same pull as a color screen over type.

Color and Ethics

Color does not seem to affect greatly how readers feel about the ethical quality of a newspaper, nor does it strongly affect the readers' opinion of a newspaper's value or importance. Color does make a paper appear more interesting, pleasant, exciting, and powerful.

Further Study

This pilot study was not intended to answer all the questions the industry has about how to use color. We designed it only as a starting point for further research. And because so little has been done previously, we need much further research just to lay down a base of knowledge. The results of this study need to be validated with new research using slightly differing methodology.

We suggest the following promising lines of inquiry:

• In a similarly well-controlled comparison, how does *bad* color compare with *good* color on some of these same tests?

• How would a page with a little less spot color compare with the heavily-colored pages used in the test?

• How does color affect the length of time spent on a story and the depth of recall of the information afterward?

• How would a larger and more representative sample of readers respond to the color test pages?

The Poynter Institute hopes that this study has provided a good beginning and inspiration for further research.

[An alternative version of this chapter appeared in Design: The Journal of the Society of Newspaper Design, No. 21 (1986) 8-15. Ed.]

Mario R. Garcia is an associate director at The Poynter Institute.

Robert Bohle is an assistant professor in the School of Mass Communications at Virginia Commonwealth University, where he teaches graphics, newspaper design, editing, and research methods. The author of From News to Newsprint, Bohle is an active workshop leader and newspaper design consultant.

Questions and Observations

1. The fact that the four leading papers listed in the first paragraph use no color may contribute to the notion that "real" newspapers print in black and white. This research project discovered that the public does not share this prejudice. How can newspaper leaders overcome this myth in their own staffs as they move toward more color?

2. Garcia and Bohle criticize "uninformed" color use. How can the industry arrive at standards (or at least general agreement) on what constitutes good color?

3. Some newspapers, among them the leaders in color, appeared on the list of newspapers using color well and also among the ranks of those using it poorly, which Garcia and Bohle interpret as disagreement on definitions among the experts. We could also interpret the paradox optimistically, that the experts think the best color practitioners do not print color as well as they should.

4. Some respondents to the questionnaire objected to "colors inappropriate to the subjects of graphics." How can we determine appropriateness to subject, which may vary culturally and regionally? Wouldn't we also expect this quality to change with fashion?

5. Some of the advertising research describes color's ability to attract attention. How can we translate this seductive feature into a tool for guiding the readers' eyes over the page? In so manipulating the readers, do we run the risk of creating a feeling of competition for their attention on what should seem a harmonious page?

6. Color and black and white differ in their ability to affect recall and depth of recall. How can we decide what we want readers to remember and in what detail? We should keep in mind that newspapers are tools for thought.

7. Chestnut, Garcia, and Bohle talk about "primitive" cultures and their supposed notions and uses of color. But most of what we think we know about primitive cultures is incomplete, mostly wrong, and colored by our own biases. "Primitives" seen from the inside are seldom primitive.

8. Just because people name blue as their favorite color does not mean they prefer a newspaper with a blue nameplate, despite *USA Today*.

9. Garcia and Bohle confess: "We know very little for certain about how people react to color." This sad admission should serve as a spur to general color research, and especially to research by journalism professors about newspaper color. The most basic questions have not yet been asked.

10. The test subjects, chosen by the newspapers themselves, proved more educated than the average newspaper reader. How can a paper choose truly representative test subjects for its own local surveys?

11. Garcia and Bohle tried to rule out volition by asking readers "where their eye first fell." Do we picture our readers as subjects responding to stimuli or as persons exercising personal choices? We should take care not to get caught up in manipulative games with our readers, who might resent such attempts at mind control. People, not white mice, read newspapers.

12. The interviewers told the subjects that "content was not necessarily important," and should be disregarded. This injunction might remind us of Tolstoy's fraternity initiation, when he had to stand for 10 minutes in front of his brothers without once thinking of a white bear! News is primarily content, and secondarily form. No matter what you tell subjects, they still act from old habits.

13. The authors note paradoxically that "color could be seen as keeping the reader from getting right to the news." How can designers insure that color attracts the reader to the news and not elsewhere? Caveat: the manipulative use of color on news pages has profound political implications.

14. Study the researchers' 20 word pairs. What would you add to this list if you conducted this study? We might add "confusing/organized," for example.

15. In light of the tradition of "serious" newspapers printed in black and white, we might wonder at the finding that color does not seem to affect opinions negatively on the evaluative or ethical scales. How would you explain this finding? Think about the tradition, recent changes in newspapers, the role of television, the test methodology, and the sophistication of readers.

16. Color pages scored higher on "believability" in towns with color newspapers. Perhaps color distracts when it is new, and the readers settle back with the text once they get used to color.

17. The authors speculate that "older readers may find color helpful because it helps to organize the page." Perhaps the future of responsible color lies here, as a tool for helping the reader make sense of the disparate elements on the page.

18. Garcia and Bohle use the phrase "bad color" as if we all agreed on its meaning. How can we achieve some sort of consensus on what constitutes bad color? Can we define it as something more than just the opposite of "good color," about which we find no agreement either?

19. The Poynter Institute has started further research on newspaper color. What would you like to contribute to this effort?

5
Color & Street Sales

John Mauro

This survey was part of a national cooperative program to assess the effects of color versus black and white in terms of attention, recognition, and sales effect in advertising. Media General also tested effects of ROP (Run of the Press) color in coupon redemption using split-run tests. The study sought to support or reject the theory that newspaper color is more attractive to customers than black and white at the point of purchase.

The study measured sales at rack box locations in the City of Richmond and Henrico County, Virginia. Researchers interviewed adults purchasing a newspaper from a rack at all seven test locations. Generally, people in the Richmond area are exposed to color above the fold on the front page of the *News Leader* about two out of six days a week. Therefore, they expect to see black and white.

The test was conducted on Friday, June 21, 1985, from noon to 6 p.m., when the Capital edition of the *News Leader* is normally purchased. The test day was sunny and seasonally warm. The locations were selected for representative geographic distribution and high volume sales, according to the circulation department.

Two identical racks were placed side by side at each of the seven test locations, each showing the upper half of the front page. Each version was distinguishable from approximately 10 feet. The newspapers placed in the racks were identical except for two items:

(1) A photograph in the upper right-hand corner of the front page, measuring three columns by five and one-half inches, was printed in black and white on one version and in full color on the other.

(2) In the color version, two blue lines ran across the page above the photograph, sandwiching the logotype and the promos above it.

The test was designed to avoid any bias due to position. At three of the seven test locations, the newspapers with the color were put in the rack on the right side. At the remaining four locations, the newspapers with the color were put in the rack on the left side.

FIG. 5A. To test the effect of color on newsrack sales, two versions of the afternoon paper were printed: one in black and white, and one with spot color bars and a four-color photo. The two versions were placed in newsracks side by side at seven locations in and around Richmond, Virginia. At three locations, the color was in the right-side rack; in the other four, on the left.

FIG. 5B. At each of the locations, trained interviewers stood well back from the racks. After a purchase, they approached the buyer and asked a few questions. In this test, color outpulled black and white 78% to 22%.

Two experienced interviewers at each location were positioned far enough from the racks so as not to intimidate would-be purchasers. As soon as the customer made a purchase, an interviewer would ask the person to participate in the survey. If the purchaser would not participate, the interviewer still recorded which newspaper was bought (color or black and white), the location of the rack, time of purchase, sex, and race.

One hundred twenty-three newspapers were purchased. One person bought two black-and-white versions from the same box. (By the way, we saw no one putting in a quarter and taking more than one paper. In Richmond, people steal only our Sunday paper!) The team invited all 122 purchasers to be interviewed. Twenty-three refused; the main reason given was that they were in a hurry.

Of those interviewed, about half (54 percent) purchase the *News Leader* from a rack every day; 78 percent buy it three or more days per week. Most likely, they buy from different locations (58 percent), averaging nearly two different locations.

Buying Out of Habit

Three-fourths of the purchasers buy out of habit; they gave no specific further reason. Of the 25 percent who had a specific reason for buying that particular issue of the newspaper, one-half had a particular story in mind, notably news of the TWA Flight 847 hostage situation, which, at the time of the study, was very hot news.

Eighty percent of the buyers read a newspaper every day. Nearly all (97 percent) read a newspaper in a week. Few (5 percent) read newspapers

other than *The Richmond News Leader* or the *Richmond Times-Dispatch*. Fewer than 4 out of 10 (38 percent) buyers have any newspaper home delivered. Of those who do, 81 percent subscribe to the weekday *Times-Dispatch*, 13 percent to the *News Leader*, 3 percent to both, and 3 percent to other newspapers. Of the copy purchased, 75 percent say other persons will also read the newspaper, notably other family members (85 percent), with the balance passed along to friends and fellow employees.

Considering that there were only 99 respondents in seven test locations, demographic characteristics were close to those of the overall community when compared with the findings of another survey conducted simultaneously. But there were a few exceptions. Rack buyers were substantially older. Somewhat more were widowed, divorced, or separated. Fewer were better educated, generally earned less money, and were employed. Surprisingly, there were no significant differences in the proportion of renters or multiple-unit dwellers.

Color Attracts

The survey showed that color outpulled black and white by 4-to-1 (78 percent to 22 percent). The survey supports the theory that color attracts, and the attraction is nearly universal. The findings imply that a color advertisement probably will generate the same attraction on a newspaper page.

One might say that color in newspapers has the interruptive value of a television commercial without the annoying side effects. It cannot be said, though, that color sells more newspapers, because the decision to purchase a newspaper was made before the prospective buyer approached the newspaper rack. Something else brought buyers to this point. Once gotten there and given a choice of black and white or color, they opted for color.

Color in Ads

Another test was conducted one month later, in July 1985, to ascertain if color in advertising performs better than black and white in coupon redemption. A pure "A/B split" was used, in which half the copies were printed in color, with the other half in black and white. Black and white versus black and two-color versions of identical ads for cents-off on bread and sugar were published by Richmond Newspapers on the first day of the sale period. The following conditions were met:
• The two products were high-volume products.
• There was sufficient inventory of these products to minimize the possibilities of running out.

• The cents-off value was sufficiently high to stimulate sales.
• No additional advertising or point of purchase promotion was given to the two products during the time of the test.
• The sale lasted for three or four days.
• Each store provided redeemed coupons by day of the week and store location.

The 1,000-line advertisement ran in the *News Leader* and *Times-Dispatch* on Tuesday, July 16, 1985. Coupon redemption extended to Saturday, July 20, 1985. Redemption points were in all seven locations of Chuck's Super Markets. A total of 1,472 coupons redeemed over the five-day period represented a 2.6 percent redemption rate.

In the *Times-Dispatch* (the morning newspaper), the test ad ran on the lower right portion of the back page of the second section. There was only one other color ad, a full page for Crest toothpaste, on the back of the main section. This other ad had very subdued color, while the test ad was quite loud, with red and gold. The entire paper had the following sections:
Main News section (14 pages)
Area/State section (8 pages)
Sports/Classified section (12 pages)
Retirement tabloid (28 pages).

In the evening *News Leader*, the test ad ran on the lower right-hand portion of the back page of the first section. The only other color appeared on the front page of the following *Young Virginians* section; this entire page was full of color photos. The paper had the following composition:
Main News section (14 pages)
Area News and Sports section (12 pages)
Young Virginians section (6 pages)

The findings are surprising. It was expected that the color ad would significantly outperform the black and white ad, as similar studies have indicated and reason would indicate. As it turned out, there was virtually equal performance throughout by overall performance, by store location, by product, by day of week, and by newspaper.

This outcome may be explained by the following five factors:
• The offer represented a large saving to the customer.
• The advertisement was exceptional in layout, design, and size.
• The advertisement was placed in an exceptional attention-getting position on each newspaper: the back page of the first section in the evening paper, and the back page of the second section in the morning paper.
• The ad ran all day Tuesday, when the test coupons had no competition, instead of on the best food day.
• As a result, coupon redemption was exceptional for black and white or color, indeed twice the national average.

Under these conditions, it would be difficult to do much more to the black-and-white advertisement to enhance its value. In a manner of speaking, if you are already seven feet tall, what can you do to get taller?

This finding leads one to think that, if you are not sure how well your black-and-white ad attracts attention, newspaper color buys the insurance you need. But if the ad is already powerful in black and white, color is not necessary.

Not considering black and white versus color, the evening newspaper outperformed the morning newspaper by 26 percent overall. This fact is not surprising because the evening newspaper concentrates more circulation in the area where the test stores are located, while the morning newspaper fans out farther. In stores farther out from the central area, the morning newspaper outperformed the evening newspaper. Sugar outperformed bread, as expected. Coupon redemption was highest on the peak shopping day, in this case Thursday, also as expected.

Color Expectations

From past research, we know that the public does not perceive color in newspapers as we professionals do. The public does not expect newspaper color to be as good as magazine color. People do not put the two side by side for comparison.

Measuring reader attitudes over the long term, we discovered that newspapers get an A-plus on graphics, readability, and ease of finding features. This attitude has not changed, at least not over the past 10 years. Does this finding mean that color improvements should not be made? Of course not. The more attractive, the more pleasing to the eye, the more likely we are to attract and retain readers.

Color enhances the appearance of a newspaper. But, more importantly, the reader needs assurance that newspapers provide a fair balance of reporting both sides of an issue. Readers have also told us that they want a newspaper to look like a newspaper. If we make newspapers look like magazines, the public will read us like magazines: once a week or once a month! Readers have told us that they want a high story count on page one. Although they are somewhat irritated at jumping stories, they read them anyway. Readers opt first for news (local, state, national, and international), and then for features for personal entertainment and daily planning.

John Mauro was the director of research at Media General Inc. of Richmond, Virginia until his recent retirement. He has been engaged in newspaper research since 1946 and was winner of the 1974 Sidney S. Goldish Award for significant, continuing contributions to newspaper research. Mr. Mauro has taught as an adjunct professor at Syracuse and Virginia Commonwealth universities.

Questions and Observations

1. Study the demographic data on the 99 respondents. Can we generalize on rack buyers from this sample? Are street editions aimed at the right people, using the right tactics?

2. Mauro notes that respondents had already decided to buy a paper from the rack. How could we design a test to see if color attracts potential buyers to the rack before they decide to buy?

3. Although we might hesitate to generalize from ad research to newspaper practice, the coupon test suggests that content is more important than form. Put another way, we could say that a good graphic presenting a good deal needs no color. Perhaps we need to repeat the test with a so-so bargain on a dull day.

4. Mauro says: "The public does not perceive color in newspapers as we professionals do. The public does not expect newspaper color to be as good as magazine color." If the public does not have high expectations of newspaper color, why should we spend the money to achieve magazine color? Or should newspapers attempt to raise the public's expectations in a time of rising technology and competition?

5. The readers quoted seem to hold traditional values for newspapers: solid reporting, fair coverage, variety, and a certain look. Perhaps the old journalistic verities are not so old-fashioned after all. How can designers and editors keep the old journalism in mind as they advance into the new color?

6

Tips for Designing with Color

Mario R. Garcia

So far in this book, we have attempted to present various aspects of color based on the latest expert opinions in the areas of perception, technology, and marketing.

In the final analysis, however, practitioners must translate the knowledge acquired here into practical applications of color as a design element.

As in other areas of design, there are no rules for effective use of color, only guidelines and recommendations. What works well for one newspaper may not serve the needs of another. The following tips result from digesting the research described earlier in this book, and applying it to everyday design.

Color as a Symbol

Artists have used colors symbolically from the beginning. In *The Elements of Color*, Johannes Itten writes that "among historical peoples, there have always been styles using colors as symbolic values only." The Chinese, for example, reserved yellow for the emperor; no one else was allowed to wear a yellow garment. For a pre-Columbian painter in Mexico, a red-clad figure represented an earth god.

We associate colors with certain products and institutions, for example, red for Coca-Cola, and blue for Pan Am. Readers of *USA Today* see the blue on the nameplate as a recognizable symbol, part of the newspaper's identity. Other newspapers have imitated *USA Today*'s nameplate style in varying degrees of blue tones, and with varying success.

FIG. 6A. This food page from the Orange County *Register* uses purple to illustrate a story about wine and food. Even though there is hardly any illustration, the page depends on color tones for impact, a clear example of using color as a design element. At the same time, the color communicates the meaning of the story (wines) instantly.

In design, a color may contribute to the symbolism of a story, perhaps green for a St. Patrick's Day feature, or purple for a page about wine and food. (Fig. 6A.)

Color and the Grid

Color can effectively create segments or structures within the page. On a feature section front with several stories related to the same topic, colors can departmentalize the materials, giving each segment a separate identity. The Dutch painter Piet Mondrian (1872-1944) probably invented this technique, using yellow, red, and blue to create a sense of equilibrium and asymmetrical balance within a rectangular shape.

Mondrian inspired one interesting approach, using color layers, as seen in the example from the Orange Country *Register* (Fig. 6B.)

Color as a Packaging Technique

Recently, more designers and editors organize long stories by segmenting them, increasing the number of points of entry on the page, and, as a result, the visual traffic. Either gray or color screens can be used behind boxed stories for a "wallpaper" or "draping" effect. This technique gives the various elements a common background that signifies togetherness. (Figs. 6C and 6D.)

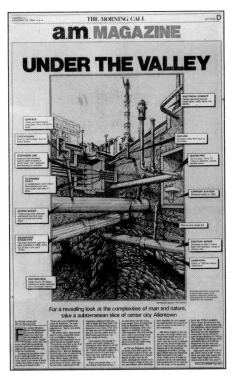

FIG. 6B. This Mondrian-inspired design appeared in the Orange County *Register*. Color layers highlight dominant colors in the photographs. The peach tone, derived from the warm colors in the large photo, is used for the three columns of text. Gray cushions the rest of the page, inspired by the blue tones in the other photographs.

FIG. 6C. A "draping" effect can unify many elements, as seen in these pages. The page to the left, from the Allentown (Pa.) *Morning Call*, has a salmon tone used as a background for the entire page. The designer has picked the blue from the photograph to highlight the dropped initial at the beginning of the article, as well as a rule that serves as a foundation to the entire page.
FIG. 6D. This example, from *The Virginian Pilot*'s Home section, uses black as a backdrop to the very colorful "tiles" in the photographs, a good solution when no one color dominates the art.

FIG. 6E. Sometimes color bars can help the indexing process, as in these promo boxes, set blue against a gray background, on page one of the *Evening Independent* from St. Petersburg, Florida.

FIG. 6G. The basic design of *Novedades* (Mexico City) incorporates color bars to move the reader from one unit to another on open pages. While the color bar normally calls attention to a headline at the top of the page, it also guides the reader to other important elements at the bottom.

FIG. 6H. This fashion page from *The Virginian Pilot* centers around a photograph in which the red on the lips of the model moves forward from the off-white of the rest of the photograph. The designer uses that red to move the reader's eye to key elements on the page.

FIG. 6F. Color bars in blue highlight the various elements on this front page from the Norwegian newspaper, *Aftenposten*. The color photographs and the effective use of background white help make this example a graphically appealing page.

Another useful packaging tool involves color rules, preferably at the top and bottom of a package, guiding the reader from beginning to end. (Figs. 6E-6G.)

Color as a Moving Force

Color can move the reader through a package. Notice how the various color elements have been "accessorized" on the page from *The Virginian-Pilot* (Fig. 6H.) Type offers another opportunity to use color to guide the reader through the contents of a page. (Fig. 6I.)

Color and Its Relationship to Gray

Shades of gray can work effectively with colors. Gray can provide visual equilibrium. In the case of photographs with bright, primary colors in them, gray can cushion the effect produced by such loud colors. (Fig. 6J.)

We must remember the special qualities of certain colors and how they project themselves on the page.

FIG. 6I. Colored type is the key to continuity of design in this special section published by the *Sarasota Herald-Tribune* to celebrate Sarasota's centennial. The soft colors compliment the main photo on the page and rest well against a white background.

FIG. 6J. Color against gray provides an interesting and effective combination, especially when many unrelated colors dominate in the photo or illustration used. Notice an effective treatment using this strategy in the promo boxes for *The Orlando Sentinel.*

FIG. 6K. White space frames each of the photographs in this photo essay page from the *Lexington Herald-Leader.* The frame, about a pica wide, helps the color photograph stand on its own, despite the gray or color background draping the page.

Even when a certain hue, such as yellow, is soft, its value (the degree of lightness or darkness) may vary. So we can talk about "soft" blues or "deep" reds.

We speak of the dynamic quality of colors, that is, how they project themselves onto the page and thus into the overall design. For example, red penetrates, moves forward fast, and indicates "hot" all over. Orange stands next to red in its penetrating ability, although it is less aggressive.

Yellow moves forward and "jumps" at the reader. Yellow is a dangerous color to use in newspapers, unless toned down. Undiluted yellow may have an overpowering effect, so that lesser elements printed in yellow (perhaps promos or the screen behind the index) take center stage, while more important elements dance in the chorus.

Green presents similar, but slightly lesser, dangers. However, unlike yellow, green is static. Translated to

design, static means "anchoring." A green screen holds the entire package down like a rock. Green bars work well, especially around photo packages where green prevails in the photographs.

Blue is probably the safest color to use. It moves forward, but also has a steady equilibrium about it. Its cool temperature tends to soothe readers.

Color and Its Relationship to White

Many of the best color pages in-

FIG. 6L. White space forms a perfect background to set off the many illustrations in this page from the Allentown *Morning Call*. For illustrations as intricate as these, a white background serves best to cushion them on the page.

FIG. 6M. Informational graphics can use color not just to attract the reader's eye, but also to provide a dominant center of visual impact on the page, as in this illustration from the *St. Petersburg Times*. Notice the gradation of colors from yellow to orange to red, then three tones of blue.

FIG. 6N. This front page from the *St. Petersburg Times* shows how color tones can enhance an informational graphic that relies entirely on bars for its impact. Gray forms an effective background tone for the index box to the right of the page. In this case, gray provides a more neutral background than one of the colors already used in the informational graphic.

---

clude some white space. White proves especially effective for framing color photos, as in the example from the *Lexington Herald-Leader*. (Fig. 6K.)

Sometimes a white background works best for a poster page when the color in the illustations is very dominant and detailed, as in the section front designed by Ken Raniere for the Allentown (Pa.) *Morning Call*. (Fig. 6L.)

Color and Informational Graphics

Informational graphics provide editors and designers with tremendous opportunities to use color. When informational graphics first became a part of the daily newspaper, they usually appeared as black-and-white images. Later, as more color became available, informational graphics were often "painted" in bright greens and yellows. Today, newspapers like

the *St. Petersburg Times* approach even the simplest bar graph or chart with a sense of graphic contrast that turns informational graphics into statistical art, simply by taking hues and playing with their values. (Figs. 6M and 6N.)

Color as a Frame

The designer can intensify the impact of a color photograph by framing

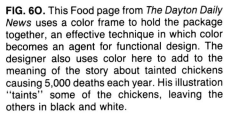

FIG. 6O. This Food page from *The Dayton Daily News* uses a color frame to hold the package together, an effective technique in which color becomes an agent for functional design. The designer also uses color here to add to the meaning of the story about tainted chickens causing 5,000 deaths each year. His illustration "taints" some of the chickens, leaving the others in black and white.

FIG. 6P. Color and type can combine in interesting ways, as seen in this Travel section front from *The Boston Globe*. Red also contributes to the eye movement from the headline (Holiday), to the initial letter, and to other elements at the bottom of the page.

it with a soft screen inspired by one of the colors dominating the photograph. The frame must be at least three picas wide and should become an accent, not a dominant element. (Fig. 6O.)

Framing boxes with color is another effective technique, made popular by *USA Today*. In an example from *The Boston Globe*, a one pica frame is recommended. (Fig. 6P.)

These tips may guide designers over those most difficult decisions involving color. Intuition plays a role, as well. If, at first, it seems like too much color, take some away. If too little, take a break; maybe it's best to leave it that way.

Ultimately, if color has contributed to making the communication process more effective, the most important of all tests has been passed.

Color and Newspapers:
A Selected Bibliography

Jo Cates and Robert Bohle

This bibliography contains the most important materials on color in general and in newspapers as of October 1986, plus any references cited elsewhere in this book. Our search concentrated on materials from the last 10 years, preferably but not exclusively in print. We have starred items we consider most helpful to non-specialists. The annotations clarify confusing or misleading titles. We would appreciate notice of any errors, of materials we have overlooked, and of items appearing subsequent to this book.

I. BOOKS AND ANNUAL PUBLICATIONS

*Agoston, G.A. *Color Theory and Its Application in Art and Design.* D. L. MacAdam, ed. New York: Springer-Verlag, 1979.

AIGA Graphic Design USA. New York: American Institute of Graphic Arts. Annual.

Art Directors Annual. New York: Art Directors Club. Dist. by Robert Silver Assoc.

Berlin, Brent and Kay, Paul. *Basic Color Terms: Their Universality and Evolution.* Berkeley: Univ. of California Press, 1969.

Birren, Faber. *Color Psychology and Color Therapy.* Reprint. Secaucus, N.J.: Citadel Press, 1984.

*Birren, Faber. *Light, Color and Environment.* Rev. ed. New York: Van Nostrand Reinhold, 1969.

Burch, R.M. *Colour Printing and Colour Printers.* New York: Garland, 1981. [Augmented 1905 edition].

*Clark, Susan. *A Selected Bibliography of Color Scanners.* Vol. I, 1980-1983. Patricia Cost, ed. Rochester: Rochester Institute of Technology, 1984.

Color in Offset Newspapers. IFRA. Darmstadt: INCA-FIEJ Research Association, 1979.

Color Theory: A Guide to Information Sources. Mary Buckley and David Baum, eds. Detroit: Gale, 1975.

*Craig, James. *Production for the Graphic Designer.* New York: Watson-Guptill, 1974. [Esp. chapter on "Color Printing"].

*Crow, Wendell C. *Communication Graphics.* Englewood Cliff, N.J.: Prentice-Hall, 1986. [Esp. chap 12].

*Evans, Ralph M. *An Introduction to Color*. New York: Wiley, 1948.

Evans, Ralph M. *The Perception of Color*. New York: Wiley, 1974.

Faiss, Fritz. *Concerning the Way of Color: An Artist's Approach*. 2nd ed. Appleton, WI: Green Hut, 1977.

*Garcia, Mario R. *Contemporary Newspaper Design: A Structural Approach*. 2nd ed. Englewood Cliffs, N.J.: Prentice-Hall, 1987. [Esp. chap. 17].

Graphis Annual. Walter Herdeg, ed. New York: Watson-Guptill.

Guptill, Arthur L. *Color Manual for Artists*. New York: Van Nostrand Reinhold, 1962.

Holmes, Nigel. *Designer's Guide to Creating Charts & Diagrams*. New York: Watson-Guptill, 1984.

*Itten, Johannes. *The Elements of Color*. Faber Birren, ed., tr. by Ernst van Hagen, New York: Van Nostrand Reinhold, 1970.

Jaensch, Erich R. *Eidetic Imagery and Typological Methods of Investigation*. 2nd ed., tr. by Oscar Oeser. New York: Harcourt Brace, 1930.

Kueppers, Harald. *The Basic Law of Color Theorey*. tr. by Roger Marcinik. Woodbury, NY: Barron's, 1982.

*Moen, Daryl R. *Newspaper Layout and Design*. Ames: Iowa State Univ. Press, 1984. [Esp. chapter 14].

*Pavey, Donald. *Colour*. London: Marshall; Los Angeles: Knapp, 1980.

Photographis. Walter Herdeg, ed. New York: Watson-Guptill. Annual.

*Sanders, Norman. *Photographing for Publication: A Guide for Photographers, Editors and Graphic Art Professionals*. New York: Bowker, 1983. [Esp. chaps 5-7].

Scott, Walter Dill. *The Psychology of Advertising*. rev. ed. Boston: Small, Maynard, 1921.

Simon, Hilda. *Color in Reproduction: Theory and Techniques for Artists and Designers*. New York: Viking Press, 1980.

Southworth, Miles. *Pocket Guide to Color Reproduction*. Rochester, N.Y.: Rochester Institute of Technology, 1979.

Stockton, James. *Designer's Guide to Color*. 2 vols. San Francisco: Chronicle Books, 1984.

Varley, Helen. *Colour*. London: Marshall, 1980.

Verity, Enid. *Color Observed*. New York: Van Nostrand Reinhold, 1980.

Weinberg, Adam D. *On the Line: The New Color Photojournalism*. Philadelphia: Univ. of Pennsylvania Press, 1986.

II. MAGAZINE, JOURNAL, AND NEWSPAPER ARTICLES

Adams, James. "When to Put Color into Advertising." *Marketing*, June 1979, pp. 50, 52, 54.

Ahearn, James. "One Step at a Time." *ASNE Bulletin*, April 1984, p. 10. [Dealing with color worries].

*Allison, Larry. "8 Affordable Steps to Color." *ASNE Bulletin*, April 1984, p. 6.

Anderson, Thelma and Dunaway, James. "Newspaper Color: It Really Works." *Editor & Publisher*, 27 Sept. 1986, pp. 1C-2C.

"ANPA Survey: Color Scanners a Growing Trend." *Editor & Publisher*, 23 March 1985, p. 33.

Archer, H.B. "Multiple Halftone Exposure Times for Three Point Control." *Technical Association of the Graphic Arts Proceedings*, 1977, pp. 184-218.

Ascher, Amalie Adler. "Color News for Mulch." *Rodale's Organic Gardening*, Oct. 1985, pp. 44ff. [It works].

Auchincloss, D. "Purpose of Color." *Graphic Arts Monthly*, Nov. 1978, pp. 46, 48.

Back, Paul. "State of Design: The Next Big Challenges—Color and Pagination." *Design: The Journal of the Society of Newspaper Design*, No. 13, Fall 1983, p. 12.

Balough, Maggie. "State of Design: One Newspaper's Commitment to Color Photography." *Design: The Journal of the Society of Newspaper Design*, No. 13, Fall 1983, p. 13.

Bellizzi, Joseph A.; Crowley, Ayn E.; and Hasty, Ronald W. "The Effects of Color in Store Design." *Journal of Retailing* 59 (Spring 1983), pp. 21-45.

Benbasat, I. and Dexter, A.S. "An Investigation of the Effectiveness of Color and Graphical Information Presentation Under Varying Time Constraints." *MIS Quarterly* 10(1985), pp. 59-83.

Bieberle, Gordon F. "Visual Impact on Your Cover." *Publishing Trade*, Sept.-Oct. 1982, pp. 21-24.

Birkett, W.B. "Design Objectives for Color Reproduction Systems." *TAGA Proceedings*, 1977, pp. 165-184.

Bjerstadt, Ake. "Warm-Cool Color Preference as Potential Personality Indicators: Preliminary Note." *Perceptual and Motor Skills* 10 (1960), pp. 31-34.

Bohle, Robert. "Readers Tell Us About Color: Poynter Institute Study Answers and Raises Questions About Color Use." *Design: The Journal of the Society of Newspaper Design*, No. 21, 1986, pp. 8-15. [Alternative version of "Research Findings" chapter in this book].

Bonnell, B. "The Colour Newspaper Advertising of American Department Stores." *Graphis* 33 (No. 191, 1977-78), pp. 194-217.

"Bridging Gap in Color Reproduction." *World-Wide Printer*, March-April 1980, p. 14. [Transparencies vs. reproduction].

Bundesen, Claus and Pedersen, Leif F. "Color Segregation and Visual Search." *Perception and Psychophysics* 33 (May 1983), pp. 487-493.

Busniakova, Marta. "Preference of Colours and Coloured Stimulus Structures Depending on Age." *Psychologia A Patopsychologia Dietata*, 12 (No. 5, 1977), pp. 401-410.

*Click, J.W. and Stempel, Guido H. III. "Reader Response to Front Pages with Four-Color Halftones." *Journalism Quarterly* 53 (Winter 1976), pp. 736-738.

"Color and the Graphic Arts: Selections from an Exhibition at the Library of Congress." *Quarterly Journal of the Library of Congress* 31 (1975), 18 pages.

"Color in Newspapers." *Graphic Arts Monthly*, Oct. 1985, pp. S10, S14, S16.

"Color in Newspapers." *News Photographer*, Dec. 1983, pp. 6-7.

Cousley, S.B. "The Impact of Color Contrast on Advertising Effectiveness." *Southern Marketing Association Conference Proceedings*, Oct. 1976, pp. 249-251.

Curtis, Richard; Denman, Bob; and Steffans, Brian. "L.A. Workshop: On Newspaper Color and Content." *Design: The Journal of the Society of Newspaper Design*, No. 14, Winter 1983, pp. 16-17.

Cvengros, Stephen F. "The Debate Over 'Correcting' Wire Color Photo Separations." *APME News*, June 1986, pp. 8-9.

"Daily Develops Way to Improve Color Wirephoto Reproduction." *presstime*, June 1985, p. 76.

Deitch, Joseph. "Not Much Color in N.Y.C. Dailies." *Editor & Publisher*, 23 Nov. 1985, pp. 16-17, 37.

Doherty, Edward J. "*USA Today* and Color: 'Nothing to Panic Over.'" *ASNE Bulletin*, April 1984, pp. 9-10.

*Donath, Bob. "Fine-Tuning Creative Tactics: How Koppers Co. Diagnoses Ad Performance with Readership Score Analysis." *Business Marketing*, Sept. 1984, pp. 128, 130, 132, 136.

Dunphy, Joseph, *et al.* "Paper Chemicals Put Brightness on Page One." *Chemical Week*, 26 Feb. 1986, pp. 20-23.

Dusky, Lorraine. "Startling New Theories on Light and Color." *Popular Mechanics*, Sept. 1978, pp. 80-81, 184, 186, 188.

Edmonson, R.J. "Success Abroad Sparks U.S. Boom in Electronic Color Scanners." *Graphic Arts Monthly*, June 1979, pp. 36-42.

*"E&P 22nd Annual Color Issue." *Editor & Publisher*, 30 Sept. 1978.

*"E&P 23rd Annual Color Issue." *Editor & Publisher*, 29 Sept. 1979.

*"E&P 24th Annual Color Awards." *Editor & Publisher*, 27 Sept. 1980.

*"E&P Color Issue." *Editor & Publisher*, 26 Sept. 1981.

*"E&P Annual Color Issue." *Editor & Publisher*, 24 Sept. 1983.

*"E&P Annual Color Issue." *Editor & Publisher*, 29 Sept. 1984.

*"E&P Newspaper Color Section." *Editor & Publisher*, 28 Sept. 1985.

*"E&P Color Section." *Editor & Publisher*, 27 Sept. 1986.

*English, Roni M. "Standardizing Newspaper Color: A Spectrum of Challenges." *INAME News*, April 1985, pp. 7-10. [Reader response to color.]

Evans, Bill. "Newspaper Color: Differences Are More Style Than Substance." *APME News*, Aug.-Sept. 1986, pp. 13-15.

*Eysenck, H.J. "A Critical and Experimental Study of Colour Preferences." *American Journal of Psychology* 54 (July 1941), pp. 385-394. [Race and sex differences].

Fannin, Rebecca. "Newspapers Repackage for National Ads." *Marketing and Media Decisions*, April 1982, pp. 59-61, 128-135.

Fogel, Robin. "Business Pages Don't Have to Look Gray." *Design: The Journal of the Society of Newspaper Design*, No. 16, Summer 1984, pp. 28-29.

Fuchs, Boris. "Readers in the U.S.A. Prefer Colourful Newspapers." *Newspaper Techniques*, Feb. 1986, pp. 14-19. [Report on Poynter Color Symposium].

Gaines, Rosslyn and Little, Angela C. "Developmental Color Perception." *Journal of Experimental Child Psychology* 20 (December 1975), pp. 465-486.

"Gannett, 54 Papers Link for Color Ads." *Advertising Age*, 4 Feb. 1985, p. 66.

Garneau, George. "Color Quality Control: How It's Done at *USA Today*." *Editor & Publisher*, 19 Jan. 1985, pp. 11, 22-23.

Garneau, George. "Computer Analysis of Color Promotes Better Quality." *Editor & Publisher*, 27 Sept. 1986, p. 14C.

Garneau, George. "The Goss Press of the Future." *Editor & Publisher*, 27 Sept. 1986, pp. 5C, 18C.

Garneau, George. "Want to Improve your Newspaper's Color? A Color Scanner Will Help You Do It." *Editor & Publisher*, 12 Jan. 1985, pp. 20-22.

Garth, Alan. "Bright Future for Full Colour." *Marketing*, 20 Jan. 1983, pp. 32-34.

Geraci, Philip C. "Comparison of Graphic Design and Illustration Use in Three Washington, D.C. Newspapers." *Newspaper Research Journal*, 5 (Winter 1983), pp. 29-39.

Gillaspy, Jeff. "Process Color Trend Is Right Now." *APME News*, Sept. 1977, p. 14.

Gloede, William F. "Newspapers Eyeing Color." *Advertising Age*, 1 Oct. 1984, p. 68.

Gloede, William F. "Newspapers: Technology Transforms Production and Package." *Advertising Age*, 23 Jan. 1986, pp. 20, 22.

Goodacre, Clive. "New Developments in Color Scanner Systems." *Export Grafics USA*, Sept. 1982, pp. 8-10, 31.

Goodstein, David H. "Happy Birthday, Electronic Color." *Graphic Arts Monthly*, May 1982, pp. 100-110. [Good overview].

Green, Ronald E. "The Persuasive Properties of Color." *Marketing Communications*, Oct. 1984, pp. 50-54.

Guest, Lester. "Status Enhancement as a Function of Color in Advertising." *Journal of Advertising Research*, June 1966, pp. 40-44. [Color not more prestigious].

Guzda, M.K. "Does Your Color Measure Up?" *Editor & Publisher*, 4 May 1985, pp. 24-25.

Guzda, M.K. "Understanding Color is the Key." *Editor & Publisher*, 4 May 1985, pp. 25, 128.

Hartman, Barrie. "Are People Buying Us for Color—or Words?" *ASNE Bulletin*, April 1984, p. 11.

Healey, Gerald B. "An Eye for Color." *Editor & Publisher*, 26 June 1976, pp. 27-28.

Hendon, Donald W. "How Mechanical Factors Affect Ad Perception." *Journal of Advertising Research*, August 1973, pp. 39-45. [Color better for attention, B&W for recall].

Hoyt-Biga, Evelyn. "Color, Color, Color, Color." *Quill and Scroll*, Dec.-Jan. 1985/86, pp. 8-11.

Jaspert, W.P. "Weekend Color Helps Newspaper Gain German Prestige Advertising." *Newspaper Production*, April 1976, pp. 19, 35.

Johnstone, Peter. "From Camera to Scanner and Beyond," *Graphic Arts Monthly*, Oct. 1983, pp. 45-46, 49-50, 52.

Karmel, Pepe. "Raising a Hue: The New Color." *Art in America*, Jan. 1982, pp. 27-31.

Katzman, Nathan and Nyenhuis, James. "Color vs. Black-and-White Effects on Learning, Opinion and Attention." *AV Communication Review*, Spring 1972, pp. 16-28.

Kehres, L. "Camera Clinic: Step-by-Step Guide to Indirect Color Separations." *In-Plant Reproductions*, Feb. 1980, pp. 10-11.

Kelly, Wayne. "Newspapers Can Use Color Inappropriately." *Editor & Publisher*, 22 Oct. 1983, p. 24.

Kruglinski, Paul. "Special Reports: Inks." *presstime*, Oct. 1985, pp. 26-32.

Lester, Paul. "Videotex Design: Color Graphics Versus Text Only." *Videodisc and Optical Disk*, Nov./Dec. 1984, pp. 468-474.

*Lockwood, Robert and Miller, Edward. "A Few of Us Print Color, But Most of Us Print 'Colorful Mush.'" *ASNE Bulletin*, April 1984, pp. 3-5.

*"The Marriage of Statistics and Images," *Step-By-Step Graphics*, Nov.-Dec. 1985, pp. 26-34.

Mayer, Bill. "Color: A Way of Life." *APME News*, Dec. 1977, p. 19.

Moen, Daryl. "Don't Make It Color for Color's Sake." *Design: The Journal of the Society of Newspaper Design*, No. 21, 1986, p. 15.

Morse, Nancy M. "When Choosing Color, Let the User Beware." *The Professional Communicator*, June-July 1986, pp. 12-13.

Nakshian, Jacob S. "The Effects of Red and Green Surroundings on Behavior." *The Journal of General Psychology* 70 (1964), pp. 143-66. [Skeptical about color and emotion].

*Newsom, D. Earl. "Split Run Research Will Find Out What People Read." *Publisher's Auxiliary*, 24 Dec. 1976, p. 11. [How to test reader response to color].

O'Brien, H. "A New Page in the History of Newspapers." *Marketing and Media Decisions*, July 1984, pp. 170-171.

Parish, S.C. "Characteristics of the Original in Colour Reproduction." *Professional Printer*, March 1977, p. 2.

Peretti, Peter O. "Color-Mood Associations in Young Adults." *Perceptual and Motor Skills* 39 (1974), pp. 715-18.

Phillips, John. "Scanning the Marketplace for Color Profit Potential." *Printing Impressions*, Jan. 1984, pp. 18H-18I.

Radolf, Andrew. "Standardization of Color." *Editor & Publisher*, 26 Jan. 1985, pp. 8-9. [NAB and ANPA programs].

Ray, Michael L.; Sawyer, Alan G.; and Strong, Edward C. "Frequency Effects Revisited." *Journal of Advertising Research*, February 1971, pp. 14-20. [B&W ad has better depth of recall].

Raymond, Douglas E. "Direct-Mail, P-O-P, Packaging Call for Color." *Advertising and Sales Promotion*, Oct. 1971, p. 46. [Color associations for promotions].

"Readers and Advertisers Want More, Better Color." *presstime*, July 1986, pp. 50-51.

Reece, Chuck. "NAB to Publishers: Color Ads or Fade." *Adweek*, 20 May 1985, p. 17.

Rexroad, Carl. "Medium Size, Smaller Dailies in U.S. Making More Use of Color, Graphics." *APME News*, Oct. 1983, pp. 16-17.

Rinehart, William D. "To Add 'Snap' to Red Spot Color, Mix Yellow with Magenta." *presstime*, Jan. 1985, p. 61.

Robison, James T. "It's Time to Raise Warning Flags." *ASNE Bulletin*, April 1984, pp. 10-11. [Bad color cheapens news].

Rosenthal, Steve. "The Color Macintosh Is Here." *A-Plus*, May 1986, pp. 129-132.

Rudoman, Bennett. "Scanning the Possibility of Digitized Color Separations." *Printing Impressions*, August 1983, pp. 20T-20U.

Sachrow, Stanley. "Packaging—How Color Can Help Sell Your Product." *Product Management*, January 1975, pp. 34-36.

Samuels, S. Jay. "Attentional Process in Reading: the Effect of Pictures on the Acquisition of Reading Responses," *Journal of Educational Psychology*, 58 (1967), pp. 337-342. [Pictures distract poor readers].

*Sanford, R. "Reproducing Color Copy," *Flexographic Technical Journal*, March-April 1980, pp. 8-13. [Color separation].

Schaninger, C.M. "The Emotional Value of Different Color Combinations." *American Marketing Association Proceedings*, No. 41, 1977, pp. 23-26. [Some differences in color response based on sex].

Schneider, A.G. "Scanner vs. Camera." *Art Product News*, Nov.-Dec. 1979, p.18. [Color separation].

Schoonmaker, Mary Ellen. "The Color Craze." *Columbia Journalism Review*, March-April 1983, pp. 35-37

Schweiger, Gunter C. and Hruschka, Harald. "Analysis of Advertising Inquiries." *Journal of Advertising Research*, Oct. 1980, pp. 37-39. [Color increased inquiries].

Seelye, Katharine. "Al Neuharth's Technicolor Baby." *Columbia Journalism Review*, March-April 1983, pp. 27-35. [On *USA Today*].

Shaw, David. "Newspapers Going for a New Look; More Color, Graphics." *Los Angeles Times*, 13 March 1986, sec. 1, pp. 14, 29.

Shaw, David. "Some Newspapers Want to Stay Just Plain Read; The Trend Toward Color." *Los Angeles Times*, 14 March 1986, sec. 1, pp. 1, 20.

*Shepperd, Wayne. "And...Now...the Problems." *ASNE Bulletin*, April 1984, p. 7. [Color photo problems].

Smets, Gerda. "Time Expression of Red and Blue." *Perceptual and Motor Skills*, 29 (1969), pp. 511-14. [Red and blue affect time sense].

Souter, John and Fisch, Richard. "Setting Color Standards." *Graphic Arts Monthly*, Oct. 1985, pp. 130-132, 134, 138.

Southworth, Miles. "Color Separation Darkroom Problems (1)." *Printing Impressions*, Jan. 1976, pp. 67-68.

Southworth, Miles. "Color Separation Darkroom Problems (2)." *Printing Impressions*, Feb. 1976, pp. 73-74.

Southworth, Miles. "No Separation Method Suits All Needs." *Printing Impressions*, March 1977, p. 9.

Sparkman, Richard, Jr. and Austin, Larry M. "The Effect on Sales of Color in Newspaper Advertisements." *Journal of Advertising*, 9 (1980), pp. 39-42. [Color has 41% advantage over B&W].

Spear, Ernie. "Take Advantage of their Flexibility to Get Maximum Advertising Results." *Sales and Marketing Management in Canada*, November 1982, pp. 14, 16. [Use spot color sparingly].

"Starch: Bleed Ads Score Higher; Right and Left Pages Noted Equally." *Editor & Publisher*, 4 April, 1981, p. 17.

Stein, M.L. "Color in California." *Editor & Publisher*, 29 Sept. 1984, pp. 9, 50. [Survey of California papers].

"Survey Reveals that More Newspapers Are Using More Scanners More Often." *presstime*, March 1985, p. 56.

Tannenbaum, Percy H. and McLeod, Jack H. "Public Images of Mass Media Institutions," in Wayne A. Danielson, ed., *Paul J. Deutschmann Memorial Papers in Mass Communications Research*. Cincinnati: Scripps-Howard Research, December 1963, pp. 51-60.

Thompson, Gene. "Readership Studies—What Part They Play in Publication Selection." *Marketing and Media Decisions*, April 1983, p. 84, 87. [Warnings before you do your own color vs. B&W tests].

Torres, Dorothy. "'Most Editors are Afraid.'" *ASNE Bulletin*, April 1984, p. 8. [Using color bravely].

Toufexis, Anastasia. "The Bluing of America," *Time*, 18 July 1983, p. 62. [Color in everyday life].

Valladares, Daz. "A Harder Sell in the Colour Pages." *Marketing*, 18 March 1982, pp. 71-72.

Vernon, M.D. "The Value of Pictorial Illustration." *British Journal of Educational Psychology* 2 (1953), p. 180. [Color illustration improves recall].

Warden, C.J. and Flynn, E.L. "The Effect of Color on Apparent Size and Weight." *American Journal of Psychology* 39 (July 1926), pp. 398-401.

Weisberger, Fran. "Technological Advancements in Newspapers." *Marketing and Media Decisions*, Aug. 1985, pp. 80, 82.

Werley, Robert. "A Photo Committee Report: How Three Papers Get Good Color." *APME News*, Oct. 1977, p. 14.

Wexner, Lois B. "The Degree to Which Colors (Hues) Are Associated with Mood-Tones." *Journal of Applied Psychology* 38 (1954), pp. 432-435.

Wilken, E. "New Proofing System in Action: Raster Display Processor." *Graphic Arts Monthly*, Aug. 1983, pp. 106-08.

Williams, L. "The Effect of Target Specification on Objects Fixated During Visual Search." *Perception and Psychophysics* 1 (1966), pp. 315-318. [Color and organization].

Wilson, Glenn D. "Arousal Properties of Red versus Green." *Perceptual and Motor Skills* 23 (1966), pp. 947-49.

"Wilson Punctures Ad Readership Myth." *Advertising Age*, 15 Jan. 1979, p. 63.

III. STUDIES, REPORTS, AND DISSERTATIONS

Clark, Ruth. *Relating to Readers in the '80s.* Washington, D.C.: ASNE, 1984.

*Click, J.W. and and Stempel, Guido H. III. "Reader Response to Front Pages with Modular Format and Color." *ANPA News Research Report*, No. 35, 29 July 1982, pp. 2-5.

"Color It Green." Monograph. *Independent, Press-Telegram*, Long Beach, Calif., 1968. [Cost effectiveness of color ads.]

"Effect of Colored-Textured Paper Stock on Self-Mailer Response." *Direct Response Research Reports*, Tests 78101, 79101, 79021. Richmond, Va., Diller Paper Co., no date.

Guldin, Mark F. "Activity in Color, Illustration, and Message as an Indicator of Advertisement Effectiveness." Ph.D. dissertation, University of Iowa, 1968. *Dissertation Abstracts* 29 (01A, 1968) p. 223. [Color superior to illustration].

"Newspaper Black & White vs. Color Coupon Test." *Media General Research*, August 1985. 10pp. [Color and B&W equal].

Pipps, Val Steven. "Measuring the Effects of Newspaper Graphic Elements on Reader Satisfaction with a Redesigned Newspaper Using Two Methodologies." Ph.D. dissertation, Syracuse University, 1985. *Dissertation Abstracts* 46 (09-A, 1985), p. 2476.

Pritchett, Thomas K. "An Experimental Test of the Impact of Color as an Attention Producing Device in Magazine Advertising." D.B.A. dissertation, Florida State Univ., 1982. *Dissertation Abstracts*, 43 (02-A, Aug. 1982), p. 535 [Color superior, but diminished by surrounding color].

"Skip the Surveys. Stick to the Cash Register." Monograph. *Independent, Press-Telegram*, Long Beach, Calif., 1978. [Color worth the cost].

Sloane, Patricia. "A Comparative Analysis and Critique of Color Theory." Ph.D. dissertation, New York Univ., 1972. *Dissertation Abstracts*, 33 (O7-A, 1972), p. 3504. [Nearly everything about color and a complete bibliography].

"Survey of Front Page Color vs. B&W: *Richmond News Leader*," *Media General Research*, June 1985. [Color outpulled B&W 4 to 1 in racks].

Tobin, Nancy. "Understanding Changes in the Growth and Shape of Newspaper Art Departments." Survey prepared for the Society of Newspaper Design, October, 1985.

*"A White Paper on Newspaper Color." George Sweers, ed. National Press Photographers Association, 1985. [15 basic articles.]

IV. PERIODICALS

Advertising Age
AIGA
Art Direction
American Printer
Communication Arts
Computer Graphics World
*Design
Design: The Journal of the Society of Newspaper Design
*Editor & Publisher
Folio
Graphic Arts Abstracts
Graphic Arts Monthly
Graphic Design USA
Graphis
How: The Magazine of Ideas and Techniques
IFRA Newspaper Techniques
In House Graphics
News Design and Graphics
News Photographer
*presstime
Print
Step-By-Step Graphics

Jo Cates is chief librarian of The Poynter Institute for Media Studies. She compiles bibliographies for all Institute publications and writes articles on library management.

Bob Bohle is an assistant professor in the School of Mass Communications at Virginia Commonwealth University.

Color Symposium Speakers

N. Christian Anderson, editor, Orange County, Cal. *Register.*
Nanette Bisher, assistant managing editor, Orange County *Register.*
Dr. Robert Bohle, assistant professor of mass communications, Virginia Commonwealth University.
Dr. Robert W. Chestnut, vice president and director of research, Ted Bates Worldwide Inc., New York City.
Michael F. Foley, managing editor, *St. Petersburg Times.*
Dr. Mario R. Garcia, associate director, The Poynter Institute for Media Studies.
John S. Garvey, vice president, *USA Today.*
William Howard, former color lab supervisor, *St. Petersburg Times.*
Leo L. Kubiet, advertising director, *St. Petersburg Times.*
John Mauro, director of research, Media General Inc., Richmond, Va.
Ken Raniere, freelance artist, formerly of *Newsweek* and the Allentown *Morning Call.*
Randy Stano, graphics director for editorial design, *The Miami Herald.*
Dr. Miguel Urabayen, professor of journalism amd mass communications, University of Navarra, Pamplona, Spain.
John N. Walston, deputy managing editor for news, *USA Today.*

Participants

Roy Appleton Sr., general manager, *Denton* (Tex.) *Record.*
Andrew Barnes, editor and president, *St. Petersburg Times.*
Desa Belyea, assistant managing editor, *The Fresno Bee.*
Timothy Bitney, assistant managing editor for graphics, *Minneapolis Star-Tribune.*
Jim Bye, photo editor, *Virginian-Pilot* and *Ledger-Star*, Norfolk, Va.
Mike Campbell, assistant managing editor, *Anchorage Daily News.*
Dierck Casselman, graphics director, *Rochester Democrat & Chronicle.*
Jim Chambers, design editor, *The Times*, Hammond, In.
Brian Clark, photo coordinator, *Kitchener-Waterloo Record*, Ontario.
Randy Cochran, graphics editor, *Orlando Sentinel.*
Bobby Coker, newsphoto chief, *Orlando Sentinel.*
Will Counts, professor of journalism, Indiana University.
Dave Doucette, editor, *Salinas Californian.*
Robert Eisner, senior art director, *Newsday.*
Dana Ewell, news editor, *Herald & Review*, Decatur, Ill.
Dr. Don Fry, associate director, The Poynter Institute.
Boris Fuchs, research director, IFRA Institute, Darmstadt, Germany.
Ann Green, news editor, *Messenger-Inquirer*, Owensboro, Ky.
Robert Hart, photo editor, *Times Picayune*, New Orleans, La.
Andrew Harteveld, production manager, *The Washington Post.*
Richard Haydon, assistant trends editor, *Palm Beach Evening Times.*
Ed Henninger, assistant managing editor, *Dayton Daily News.*
Gary Hoenig, assistant managing editor for art, *Newsday.*
Scott Honeyman, assistant managing editor, *Ottawa Citizen*, Ontario.
J. Ford Huffman, managing editor for features and graphics, Gannett News Service.
John Irvin, production manager, *St. Petersburg Times.*
Michael Keegan, assistant managing editor for news art, *The Washington Post.*
Billie M. Keirstead, assistant director for graphics, The Poynter Institute.
Thomas Kramer, professor, Los Angeles Pierce College.
Jim Mazzotta, graphics director, *Fort Myers News Press.*
Robert G. Miller, assistant managing editor, *Palm Beach Evening Times.*
Daryl Moen, professor of journalism, University of Missouri-Columbia.
William Newton, art director, *The Record*, Hackensack, N.J.
Jack Norton, assistant lifestyles editor, *Richmond Times-Dispatch.*
Ronald Norvelle, professor of journalism, Florida A&M University.
Lynne Perri, graphics editor, *Tampa Tribune.*
Sue Reisinger, managing editor, *The Miami News.*
Steve Rice, assistant managing editor for graphics, *The Miami Herald.*
William Rinehart, vice president, technical division, ANPA.
Gil Roschuni, manager of research and development, *The Washington Times.*
Bob Schaad, operations manager, *Asbury Park Press*, N.J.
Raleigh Schein, director of advertising art, *The Washington Post.*
Warren Skipper, quality assurance coordinator, *Orlando Sentinel.*
Becky Smith, associate director, American Press Institute.
Brian Steffans, news editor for graphics, *San Diego Union.*
Tony Sutton, managing director, *Freelance Editors*, Johannesburg, South Africa.
Andrea Wieder, graphic designer, *Newsweek.*
Paul Woodsum, supplement design supervisor, *Christian Science Monitor.*